The little Goddess book of big love ideas

Elisabeth Wilson

Acknowledgements
Infinite ideas would like to thank the following authors for their contributions to this book: Peter Cross, Sabina Dosani, Helena Frith Powell, Lisa Helmanis, Marcelle Perks and Elisabeth Wilson.

First published in 2009 by
The Infinite Ideas Company Limited
36 St Giles
Oxford, OX1 3LD
United Kingdom
www.infideas.com

A CIP catalogue record for this book is available from the British Library

ISBN: 978-1-905940-89-9

Brand and product names are trademarks or registered trademarks of their respective owners.

Designed and typeset by Baseline Arts Ltd, Oxford
Printed in China

The little Goddess book of big love ideas

Brilliant ideas

Re-energise your sex life

The path of true love

We ignore our love and sex lives at our peril. Our sexuality is linked to our creativity, drive, self-esteem and personal happiness. When we neglect sex and love, we close down to a lot more than just the success of our relationships. You don't need a partner to be a love goddess, as you'll find out if you read on. And if you might as well be single for all the good being hitched is to nurturing your inner love goddess, well, there are some ideas here that will help with that, too. Whether you want to find a man, reinvigorate an existing relationship or need help with getting over a break-up this little book should have all the ideas you need to make sure your love life is a happy one.

'There are two kinds of women: those who want power in the world, and those who want power in bed.'
JAQUELINE KENNEDY ONASSIS

Jump start your love life

Have you got what it takes to be a lover?

According to the god of human relationships, psychologist John Gottman, there are several characteristics that good couples share which set them apart from couples who are likely to split. Pick the scenario that best describes your partnership style *most* of the time.

1. How easy do you find it to apologise to your partner after a fight?

- ■ a. Very easy. I make a real effort to see where they are coming from and if there's any area where I am at blame, I'm happy to apologise first.
- ■ b. Difficult. I know it takes two, but the truth is that it's his fault nearly all of the time.

2. My partner is still very hurt by some things I said to him years ago:

- ■ a. Maybe but he doesn't say.
- ■ b. Yes, every time we fight he brings it up again.

3. When we aren't getting on:
- ■ a. It's not too long before one of us cracks and gives the other a hug.
- ■ b. We avoid each other completely. We can't even bear to be in the same room.

4. We're the kind of couple:
- ■ a. Who talk all the time even when we're not getting on.
- ■ b. Who can go days without speaking to each other. We retreat into our shells.

5. When one of us has a problem:
- ■ a. We will tell the other and try to work it out together.
- ■ b. We solve it alone for the most part – and even resent the other one trying to understand or help.

You'll have guessed already that the 'a's demonstrate the 'right' way, the 'b's the 'wrong' way. The characteristics of lovers are

- ✿ You don't blame or criticise each other;
- ✿ You show respect for the other's viewpoints and ideas;
- ✿ You maintain physical intimacy even when you're angry with each other;
- ✿ You are emotionally available to the other person.

If you were short on 'a's – and it only takes being short on one to push a relationship into decline – start by reading ideas 11 and 13.

1. Learn from the masters

Everyone knows someone who is an incredible flirt, whose social diary always seems to need extra fold-out sections and who seems to be adored by all men, from infants to grandfathers.

Rather than make a voodoo doll of her, watch and learn: the good and the bad.

But she's so obvious!

Most women with these skills often seem transparent to other women; they seem to turn on the charm unashamedly and suck up to a man's ego without a second thought. Well: newsflash – men don't care. And more often than not, they usually don't even notice that she does it to every other guy in the office unless she is known as the 'praying mantis' and eats her partners after sex. This is because most people could do with a little extra attention in their lives. Face it, even if you know the guy in accounts flirts with every woman he meets on the stairs, it still makes your day less dreary – and that's because flirting makes life more fun.

Flirting also doesn't have to be about sex. It can just be about remembering to look up, crack a smile and not take everything so seriously. You may not have just made a connection with the love of

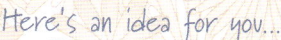

Here's an idea for you...

Look at the people who make you feel good and consider which of their qualities you like. Maybe your grandmother is a very calming person to be around because she is a great listener. Maybe your best friend is brilliant at coming up with exciting plans and making things happen. Your brother might always know how to put nervous people at ease... think about how you can adopt these easy ways of being, and look for similar traits in yourself.

your life but it's good to remember to keep things light; it's a great way to stop every date you do have from seeming like a full-scale interview.

Recognising it in action

Most good flirts have a few skills in common. Firstly, they smile a lot. That is not to say that they could be extras in *The Stepford Wives*. They just keep things upbeat, a quality that draws people whether they are friends or colleagues. Secondly, they ask questions and remember details; any good networker will tell you that this is an essential tool in making good contacts. It makes people feel appreciated, understood and special, so try and make a mental rule to ask more questions than you answer. Again, this will not turn you into some 50s housewife; it's as useful a skill in big business as it is in personal relationships. And thirdly, they often use physical contact, sometimes with themselves, and sometimes with others. Touching your hair or face gives the other person a clear signal that you are interested in them. Touching their arm or hand as you chat, taking their elbow as you go through a door – these are all ways of making people know that you are comfortable with the idea of being in their body space: or of having them in yours.

Getting flirting right for you

That isn't to say these are all right for you. If every time you see the arch-flirt you want to lock her in the stationery cupboard for pretending she can't work the photocopier when she used to work for Xerox, then you know you need to modify her tactics when you use them yourself. Maybe you can emulate the way she remembers everyone's name or gets involved with after-work activities (you might not fancy Bob in IT, but his brother could be pretty hot). It's about knowing that you might need to sharpen up your skills consciously without coming into work the next day with a completely different personality. You can use what she does wrong to help guide you: maybe her whole conversation is about the other person, which is a great way to get attention but isn't going to help move things on to the next stage. Maybe the neckline of her blouse ends around her waistband; also not a winner with every guy in town. The wise girl looks for lessons everywhere...

What comes naturally

This is why you also need to think about how you already put yourself out there. Are you always coming up with wisecracks or reminding men you meet how smart you are? Do you find yourself joking about, like you did with your male friends at college or your ex-boyfriend? Whilst this might be a great place to *get to* with a partner, it's not necessarily ideal

Defining idea...

'The mysterious is always attractive. People will always follow a veil.'
English writer and cleric BEDE JARRETT, from *The House of Gold*

when you first meet someone. Most people have a limit to how much they can take in during one sitting and definitely to how much they want to know. You may think chatting about your ex, your eating disorder and your PhD just shows your openness, but is it possible that you might be scaring people off by showing what a handful you are? Revealing yourself as you get to know one another is a much better way of allowing space for both of you to get comfortable.

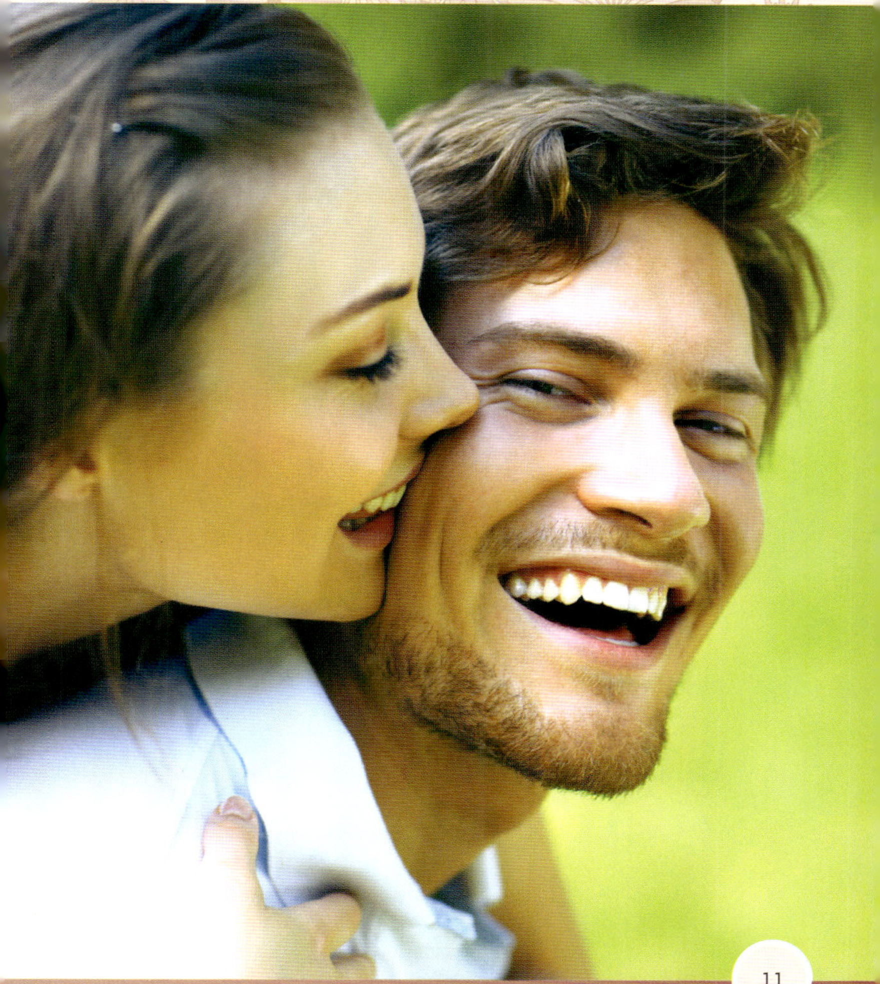

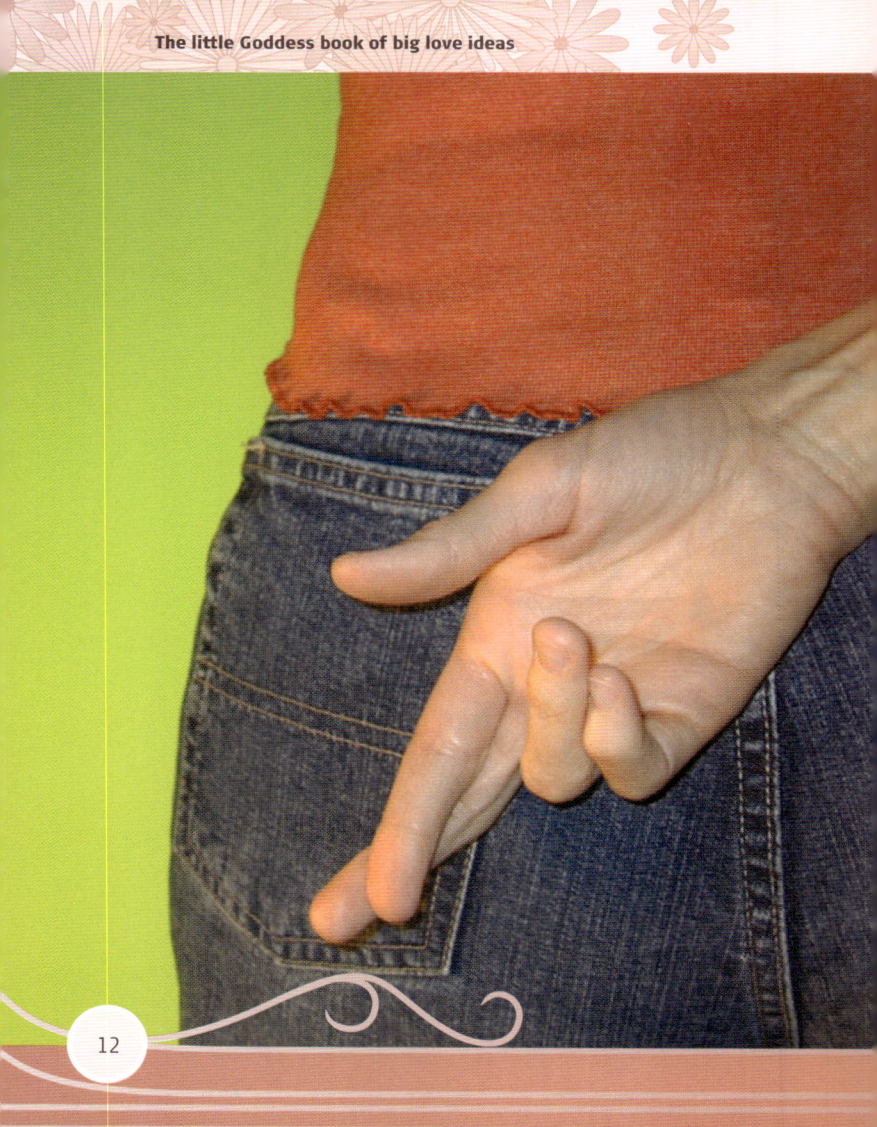

2. Being lucky at getting lucky

Got friends who seem to glide through life, people whom everyone calls 'born lucky', while nothing whatsoever seems to go your way?

Recent research has shown that there is a big difference between 'luck' and 'chance'. And you can work things out in your favour.

Chance covers things that happen to you without your input, like a hereditary illness or finding money on the street. But luck is something you can generate, by organising your life in a way that maximises every opportunity that comes along. So forget leaving your dating destiny to fate, and make sure that when good luck comes along the odds are already stacked in your favour.

Reset your mind

The first thing you need to do is change your perception of yourself as 'unlucky'. Most people can improve their chances by reprogramming their minds to think of themselves as fortunate; this means that you expect good things to happen to you and recognise opportunities as they come up, and it stops you from turning your back on chances because you believe things are too good to be true. The postman could

Here's an idea for you...

'Reframing' is a technique often employed by psychotherapists to help clients get a more positive perspective. You place the experience in another frame which fits the 'facts' of the same concrete situation equally well or even better, and thereby changes its entire meaning. It sounds a bit complicated, but it isn't, so here's an example. If you had a bad relationship that has crushed your confidence, rather than thinking you can never get over it, try thinking that you are glad to have the bad experience behind you so that you can make a better choice next time. It may feel unnatural at first, but soon choosing a better way of seeing things will become second nature.

be your perfect man but you might open the door without looking up every morning if you have decided that love is not going to come your way.

Start by resisting the temptation to relive your past failures and worries. It can dampen your spirits. Lucky people get things in perspective, look for ways to turn around disasters and expect that they will need to take chances to get what they would like out of life. When things do go right, even the little things such as finding a parking space, put that down to your skill: it will help you feel in control of your good fortune. If you find it hard to do, then jot them down on your calendar or on a notepad and see how quickly the good stuff adds up.

Become a social butterfly

Research shows that lucky people have much wider social networks, and are good at meeting new people. So get friendly; at weddings, for example, be the first to ask everyone at your table their names and whether they are friends of the bride or groom – not only will you make connections but they'll all be grateful to you for breaking the ice. You can make this easier by looking lucky. Lucky people are optimists who expect good fortune, which radiates from the way they carry themselves. If you don't do this naturally, then you can cheat: imitating their body language will fast track you to success. So avoid the folded arms, hunched shoulders, and lack of eye contact which ward people off. Be open, look up and around: how are you going to get lucky in love if you miss the opportunity to catch the eye of the handsome guy at the bar?

Defining idea...

'*How can you say luck and chance are the same thing? Chance is the first step you take, luck is what comes afterwards.*'

AMY TAN, US novelist

You know you know

Learning to trust your instincts will build your confidence and help you believe in your ability to choose what is right for you. You learn to move between 'hard knowing', which is the facts, and 'soft knowing', which is the feeling those facts give you, and you can then base your decisions on both. If you feel like something is right but can't decide, then write down the pros and cons and see if the result matches what you feel. Trying will also help you build confidence, because taking risks is essential to getting what you want. Still find it hard to take the leap? Try reading a few stars' autobiographies or watching films of their lives and see how many 'successful' people have struggled for years before getting their breaks, and also that life has ups, downs and then some more ups again. The one thing you can rely on, with luck, is that it will change.

3. Dress for success

Clothing communicates, it's a simple fact. No matter how much we regard ourselves as able to look behind the façade, one of the first signifiers we read is the packaging.

And getting yours right is key when trying to attract the right kind of attention. So exactly what is the right kind of attention?

Basically, you need to dress for the kind of man you want to appeal to, and for the kind of relationship you want to establish. Looking for a playful fling? As long as you aren't wearing a bin bag, it almost doesn't matter what you have on as you know what you want. Looking for a fellow art buff for a meaningful, life-long relationship? A spandex off-the-shoulder, thigh-skimming tube dress with some plastic wet-look boots may make other viewers at the private view think you are a performance artist. Or whatever. But you might at least earn your bus fare home.

What happened to self-respect?

Dressing to attract a man might sound like the past hundred years of women's liberation never happened. But the fact is, wearing your favourite neck-to-ankle baggy jumper may make you feel secure but it does not, in any way whatsoever, say that you are available or interested

Here's an idea for you...

Think about how your outfits are received; you may think you are being the belle of the ball but actually be coming on like a train. Consider the type of event you are going to and not just the impression you would like to make. A Halloween house party might be more suited to a fun homemade tramp outfit than an expensively hired catsuit; nothing says 'Look at me, I'm desperate!' like a bid to be super-sexy at all times. One quiet Saturday afternoon, try on lots of clothes and find something that is flattering, a little sexy and comfortable; then hang it on the back of the bedroom door as your SOS date outfit, if you get panicked. If in doubt, default to a little black dress. These have served womankind well for a very long time.

in taking things to a romantic level. Sexual attraction is an important part of finding a partner and there is nothing wrong with it: so get with the programme, have a good think about your best bits and pieces, and get them out.

Feeling fine

So how do you get the balance between what you feel comfortable in and what you think might attract the right man? Firstly, you must feel comfortable in whatever you wear, as that will help radiate confidence and an ease with your body. And don't try anything frighteningly new or too high fashion; lots of men don't care that your shoes are the latest catwalk chic, but they might care if you take a head-first dive down the club steps because you haven't mastered the art of walking in them.

A little bit of what you fancy...

It never hurts to advertise, and men are basically visual creatures, so a glimpse of a taut thigh, a crisp white shirt with a flattering neckline or a well-turned ankle in some killer heels are all great tools in your armoury. However, there is a fine line between being tantalising and being tarty. This is where the 'one or the other' rule comes into play. If you have a great décolletage, feel free to hoist your boobs up and dab some seductive scent in pertinent places. However, you may want to team that stunning, sparkly, low-cut top with some simple flattering black trousers, rather than a denim skirt the size of a belt. Even if you also have fabulous legs, too much of a good thing can slide into slut. So choose one good area and work it to its best advantage.

Now consider where you are going. A miniskirt with a black polo neck is a winning combination if you have devastating legs, but not if you have to hide all your assets under the table during dinner, with you now looking like a severe intellectual beatnik about to grill him on existentialism. The same miniskirt worn in the gods at the theatre might get the audience looking in the opposite direction from the stage. Be as objective as you can; you might love that skirt to bits, but if it's not going to work for you, put it back in the wardrobe.

Defining idea...

'**Put even the plainest woman into a beautiful dress and unconsciously she will try to live up to it.**'
LADY DUFF GORDON, 20s fashion designer

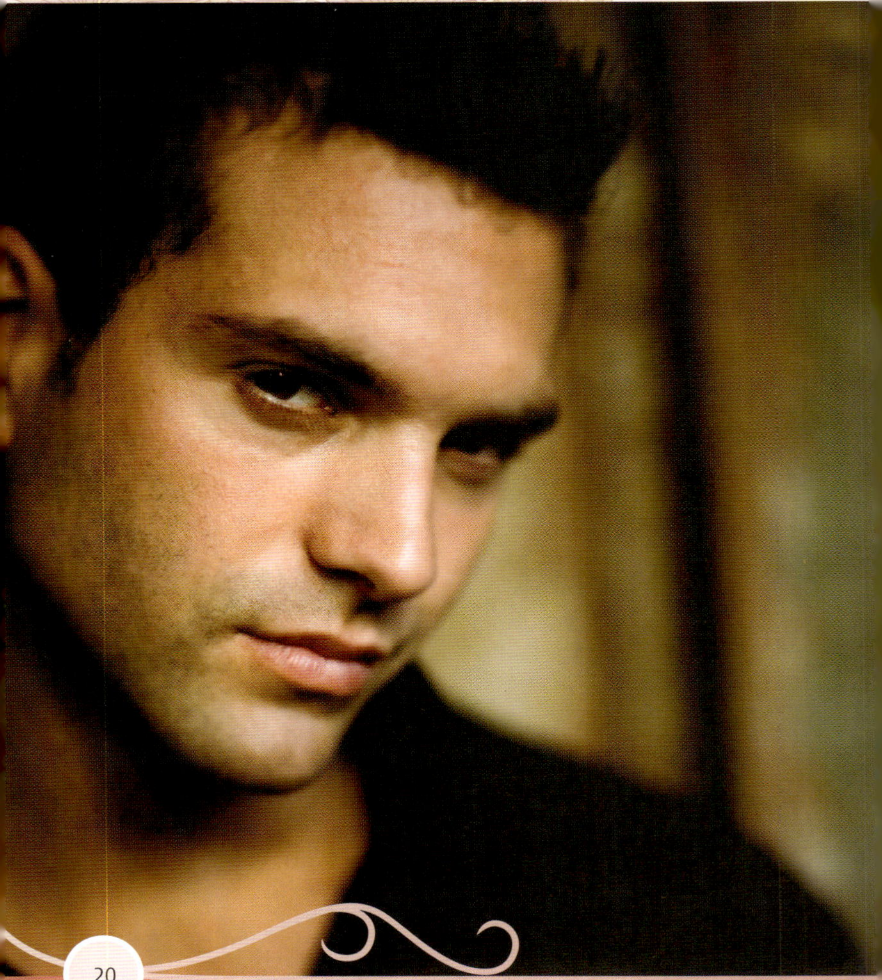

4. What men want

OK, OK, let's keep it clean, ladies. Of course, all men want that, but there are some other qualities that men are looking for too.

And there are some universal truths about what men are after, just as there are for us women.

Love

Believe it or not, men are just as keen to make a connection as women are, they are just not as likely to confuse it with good sex. Someone to share things with, rely on and love comes high on many male lists. But don't confuse the desire to love with the desire to commit: that comes later.

Desire

They want you to want them as much as they want you: and, yes, they'll want you to think about embarking on any kind of relationship. You don't have to fit the standard-issue magazine model, but they do want someone who takes pride in how she looks and feels good about her own body. There's no bigger turn-off than someone waving their cellulite in your face and telling you how hideous it is – it's called negative marketing. Stop it. You can loll about the house in no make-up and your jogging bottoms and still appear attractive if you feel good doing it, but throw in greasy hair and some whining and you are on your own.

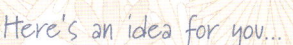

Here's an idea for you...

As well as knowing a little more about the male mind, it might be a useful exercise to work out what qualities you would ideally like – and then try and make them a reality in your next relationship rather than hoping he's a mind reader.

Happiness

Happy people are like luck magnets; everyone wants to be around them, learn their secret, get happy osmosis. And while no one can be happy all the time, your world view is pretty important. Only the creepiest of men want a depressed woman around, usually so they can feel superior. If you do have personal issues then take control of them yourself; while it's totally appropriate to share your woes with your loved one, he's not your therapist. He needs some lifting up too.

Friendship

This mustn't be confused with being like one of his mates. While men want the good stuff – loyalty, concern, fun, companionship – they don't necessarily want you outdoing them in a belching competition. And don't fake an interest in football if you haven't got any; they can always find someone else to go to the match with.

Support

Constant criticism is wearing, and an easy trap to fall into. Buoying up someone's spirits, being friendly to their friends or work associates,

these are all ways of making someone feel treasured and supported. If you can do it without them having to remind you, this will also create more trust, a vital part of feeling valued.

Defining idea...

'The male is a domestic animal which, if treated with firmness, can be trained to do most things.'
JILLY COOPER, British novelist

Sanity

What once seemed exciting and off the wall soon becomes a hideous chore. A neurotic, clingy or shouting woman might be a sexy stereotype in a film but is a nightmare to have in your life as a friend or a partner. After all, the same qualities in a man would put you off, whereas a rational person, someone you can talk to and lean on at times, generates respect and trust. Being irrational shouldn't be confused with being a challenge. Mount Everest is a challenge, but no one wants to live on it.

Challenge

So what is a good challenge? A woman who stands her ground and knows her own mind, being sharp enough to know when someone is trying it on and not becoming so acquiescent that she becomes almost invisible. If someone lets you down be clear about your feelings; men respond to direct statements (hysterics switch them off), and it shows that you think you're worth more. So they will, too.

Consideration

Shockingly, men respond to the same stuff as women! Who would have thought it? Tea in bed, making sure he has something in the fridge to eat when he gets home if he has to work late and offering to pick up medicine when he is ill… It may all seem like some weird, 50s-throwback behaviour, but these are the little acts of thoughtfulness that make a woman go weak at the knees when shown to her. The rest of the world is indifferent to his minor personal crises, so you shouldn't be. Of course, these acts should be returned, but studies show that acts of kindness make both the doer and the receiver feel good, so if you get the balance right you can both be nurtured and nurture. I can feel world peace just around the corner.

Space

Finally, men want space (and emotionally healthy women should too). Men want the room to make their own decisions, have their own private thoughts and sometimes just not think at all. Part of women's lifeblood is to always try and work out where things are at; men don't want that constant pressure. If you call him constantly at work, expect him to remember the name and love lives of your thirteen cousins *and* their cats, then you are actually expecting him to be a woman. That is what your best friend is for. Only teenage girls expect to share every intimate detail of their lives with their partners.

5. And what do you do?

Small talk. Hideous. My idea of hell is standing around a drinks party while people ask me what I do. I know that it's a useful question for generating 15 further minutes of conversation. But it's right up there with, 'Do you come here often?' in the tedium stakes as a first line.

Being sexy is not just about the way you look, smell and dress. It's about your character. One word that people associate with sexy is 'enigmatic' so try to make your first line something a bit more unusual.

In the film *White Mischief* Charles Dance clocks Greta Scacchi as they walk down the stairs. There is an obvious magnetism between them. At the bottom of the stairs he turns to her and says, "Are you going to tell your husband, or shall I?'

OK, that's fantasy not reality. But it certainly beats, 'What do you do?' in the first line stakes. I remember my father telling me off when I was about 12 for saying I was hungry. 'Don't be so banal,' he said. 'Use your imagination. Instead of saying you're hungry say: "the people in the street seem to me transformed into plates of pasta coming towards me"'. OK, so he is Italian – and mad – but you get the idea? Think slightly eccentric, quirky and charming. Instead of coming out with a line people expect you to say, dare to be different. Try starting with something that happened to you recently, or something interesting

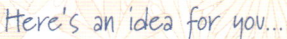

Here's an idea for you...

Jerry Hall once suggested wives should read something interesting every day so that when their husbands returned from work they had something interesting to talk about. Old-fashioned but we can all learn from the principle. If you don't do, read, see or experience anything new, you're not going to have much to talk about. So try to stay well-informed and alert, it's much sexier than ignorant.

you've read or seen in the news. The conversation will flow from whatever starting point you give it, but the person's impression of you will be different.

I can't remember the number of times I have been stuck next to people at dinner parties and they have started talking about commuting or childcare. Deadly. At first I wondered whether it was me, was I really so dull that all people could find to talk to me about was that? But when I compared notes with friends they said they'd experienced the same thing. I resolved to counter-attack. Every time someone started to talk about either topic I would say, 'Isn't it extraordinary how as soon as we get to a dinner party we start to talk about nannies or commuting? I'd much rather talk about sex, wouldn't you?' Either they start to bore the person on their other side, or you can get stuck into a gritty sexy conversation. Marvellous! Changing the tack of the conversation is good practice and just as valuable as avoiding being a dull conversationalist yourself.

Most people like to talk about themselves and have something interesting to say, even if it's not immediately apparent. In other words, you need to bring this something interesting out of them. Remember that you can

learn something from everyone.
Even if they initially come across as
the dullest person you've ever met,
try to use the time with them to
bring out their best side.

Defining idea...

**'Talking and eloquence are not the same: to
speak, and to speak well, are two things.'**

BEN JOHNSON, 17th century dramatist and wit

A good answer to the question, 'How old are you?' is, 'About your age'.
This totally floors people and also means you can avoid telling them.
Adopt this attitude when people try to make dull conversation.
Conversation is a little bit like sport: you will play to the level you find
yourself. If someone is deadly dull, you're more likely to be so yourself
and dull is NOT sexy. Either walk away from them or try to change the
subject matter. Most people are just as keen as you are to enjoy life.
They will also want to sparkle and a good conversation will help them
do that. There is nothing more infuriating than watching someone else
have the crack while you're stuck next to great bores of today talking
about trains. Now you've read this you need never go there again.
Someone totally intent on talking about trains will not be keen to spend
time with the new super-sexy conversationalist you're going to become.
You need never be on the periphery of the party again.

6. 'Let a woman be a woman, and a man be a man'

There's a bloke in the States called David Deida who has some interesting ideas as to why sex goes off the boil.

There's nothing particularly new about his ideas, but the way he packages his theories is pretty compulsive.

We're equal, but we're knackered. Even long-standing relationships are crumbling under the strain of couples overworking. Latest figures show that the divorce rate is inching towards half of all marriages.

But according to Deida, life doesn't have to be this way. Deida says women aren't drudges, but passionate, vital, thrilling creatures who given the chance should be living a life of rich emotional complexity. In order to shine, they need the love of what Deida calls 'the superior man'. A strong, focused, individual striving towards his destiny. According to Deida, when men are strong and women can rely on them, passionate intensity isn't far away. What's wrecking our sex lives, he says, is too much equality. Yes, you read that right.

'The bottom line of today's fifty–fifty relationship,' Deida continues, 'is that men and women are clinging to a politically correct sameness even in bed and that's when sexual attraction disappears. The love may be strong, but the sexual polarity fades.' According to Deida, men and

Here's an idea for you...

David Deida has written several books, including The Way of the Superior Man (for men) and It's a Guy Thing (for women). You can check out www.deida.com to see if his ideas are likely to appeal.

women have both a masculine and feminine side or 'polarity'. It's fine for men to get in touch with their feminine side (real men do cry), and women with their masculine (they're brilliant in the boardroom). She can be the breadwinner, he can look after the kids, but if they want fireworks to continue, he has to be someone she can rely on and trust, and she has to remove the shoulder pads as soon as she walks through the front door.

What's a superior man?

Deida's roots appear to be in the men's movement, the reaction to feminism, which tries to help men make sense of our crazy, mixed-up world, and their role in it. He believes that a man isn't really happy unless he's striving towards his goal, whatever that is. When he loses sight of his goal, he needs 'time out' – what in other cultures would have been called a 'vision quest' – sort of metaphorically speaking going into the desert and beating his drum until he finds his way again. Unless he finds his way he's no use to anyone, least of all his bird. This is why she has to understand the importance of his quest. She can also help him be a superior man by 'challenging him', i.e. not putting up with any shit. No lying about watching Sky Sports when he should be looking for a job, say. No nights down the pub to distract him from the fact that he

hasn't written a word of that best-selling novel. Deida calls it 'challenging'. It sounds like plain old 'nagging' to me. Anyway, there's lots in his work about how a man can become superior, but here's a couple of ways he can be superior in direct relation to the woman in his life.

Defining idea...

'**Both men and women are bisexual in the psychological sense. I shall conclude that you have decided in your own minds to make "active" coincide with "masculine" and "passive" with "feminine". But I advise against it.**'
SIGMUND FREUD

You'll know you're a superior man when you stop trying to control a woman's emotions and you listen to her. You do your best to understand her feelings and don't walk away from them. You don't offer useless advice when she wants you as a sounding board, but give her a hug. You make her laugh a lot. You're your own man. You listen, you take advice on board and then you do what you think best. You're trustworthy. You do what you say you'll do. And when you don't, you own up and take responsibility for it. You pay attention to your partner. You know that thirty minutes fully concentrating on her is worth four hours half-listening and fiddling with the remote. Got that?

Deida's ideas aren't for everyone, but I've met and interviewed couples for whom his ideas work well. The couples are equal, but they accept the sexes are different and that a man and a woman can't be everything to each other. Deida's ideas give a way of negotiating the contradictions of being a 'good bloke' and being a 'new man', which lots of men struggle with. If you can handle the New Age language, of course.

7. What's your Love Quotient score?

Imagine you're in the Mastermind chair and your specialist subject is your lover. What would be your Love Quotient (LQ) score?

It's a weird one. Ten years into our relationship and we know more about what lights the candle of the person sitting next to us at work than the person we've chosen to share our lives with.

Years ago I read something in one of John Gray's books that has saved me a lot of grief since. John Gray wrote *Men are from Mars, Women are from Venus*, and the point he made – directed at men – was simple: if your partner adores chocolates and sees them as the eternal proof that you love her, why on earth would you buy her roses? Yet the world is full of guys turning up with bunches of roses and wondering why they get thrown at their head. The moral is simple: if your lover needs chocolates to make them feel loved, give 'em chocolates. It's irrelevant whether you think a bunch of red roses is more romantic. You need to give your partner what they need or you might as well not bother.

Start looking for the 'roses instead of chocolate' trait and you'll start seeing people everywhere doing loads for their loved ones that's going unnoticed. I was quite stunned to discover that after a 'make or break' fight with my partner, all I had to do to appease him was cook him

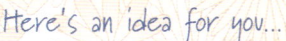

Here's an idea for you...

Feel your partner fails to listen to you? Sit them down and talk to them calmly. Huffing about or giving them the silent treatment are passive-aggressive ways of getting nowhere. You have to spell it out.

dinner. For whatever screwed up reasons of his psyche, what makes him feel loved isn't gifts of books, CDs, Thai prostitutes or weekends away – it's me getting my pinny on. And when I was upset with him, that's what he would do for me – cook me dinner. For a long time it got him nowhere, as what works for me when I feel angry is long extended conversations – and jewellery of course. Jesting aside, it wasn't until I read the John Gray book that I got it. Our LQs were low. But now when I need to butter him up I just throw a steak on the grill. And when he's upset me, he grits his teeth and gets prepared to bare his soul.

Broadly speaking, to successfully love the person we're with we need to understand what they need to feel loved. To keep their love we must give them what they need as far as possible. If you're reading this and wondering what this has to do with sex, my answer to you is, 'Duh! Just about everything.' Loads of couples are having indifferent or absolutely no sex, not because they don't spark off each other but because they haven't felt loved by their partner for years. The classic example is the bloke faced with a distraught missus, who will 'do' something practical for her – put up shelves, clean her car, pay the bills – when all she wants is a babysitter booked and a meal out.

When your lover's feeling insecure, stressed or worried, how do you make them feel safe and reassured? Does it work? If not, do you know what would? If yes, why do you withhold it from them? Do you like to play mean just for the hell of it? It might seem to work and it might keep you the 'superior' partner, but the price is high. Your partner won't be able to trust you and that sort of trust is near enough essential to keep sex hot between you when the first thrill has gone.

Defining idea...

'Sex is a conversation carried out by another means.'
PETER USTINOV

Would your lover rather have a romantic meal or a wild night out on the town as a prelude to sex? Do you occasionally indulge them, even if you'd rather do something else?

Does your partner feel closer to you when you're laughing together or being upset with you? If the answer's 'upset', do you respond in a way that seems to satisfy them or are they disappointed in you? If the answer's ' laughing', when was the last time you went out of your way to make sure you had a good laugh together?

What's your lover's favourite way of resolving a fight (not necessarily the way you always resolve it)?

These are the kind of questions you have to know the answers to. And your partner, of course, has to know what works for you. Emotionally we have to be given chocolates at least some of the time or we start to shut off from our partner and get tempted by someone who appears to offer Milk Tray on demand. If you're with someone for whom chocolate equals love, all the roses in the world won't fix your relationship or help you get good sex.

8. Just say 'no'

There's saying 'no' and there's saying 'no' nicely. Two very different things.

Every relationship has its sexual deserts when sex is off the cards. Here's how to negotiate your way through them so no one gets too hurt.

Sometimes we simply want to say 'no'. We might be tired. We might be feeling sad. We might be preoccupied with something else. If your partner approaches you and you feel ambivalent about having sex, my best advice is to go along with it for a while and try to get yourself in the mood (with their help, of course). If, however, you fail to rise onto that wave of lust, all you can do is gaze into their eyes tenderly and say, 'Sorry, it isn't working for me tonight, but I promise that tomorrow we'll do the deed.' Sex therapists pretty much agree that rejection is easier to take if there's a definite date set for a retry. As a consolation prize and to give them the human contact that we all crave (and which probably instigated their shuffle across the bed in the first place), you could hold your partner while they masturbate to orgasm. (And if you're not comfortable masturbating in front of each other, maybe you ought to think about why not. It's a useful habit.)

But what if you know that tomorrow you're not going to want to have sex either? What if this one's going to run and run? A genuine sexual desert where it's been months and months and months, and you don't

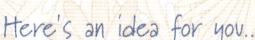

If you and your partner haven't had sex for a month, sit down, look into his/her eyes and ask why. The longer you go without sex, the easier it becomes to do without it. The more you do it, the more you'll want to.

need so much to negotiate it as buy a map and a compass and start charting the unknown continent. First things first. Do you both want to emerge from your desert and find your oasis?

'Yes' to the oasis?

Is there a medical reason that one or both of you has gone off sex? Is it because one or both of you is having a mid-life crisis? Deal with that and do the following.

'No' to the oasis

Tricky one this. You've gone off sex. You don't fancy your partner anymore. You can't be bothered to try. When they approach you, you simply don't want to do it.

Don't let sex be an *ad hoc* arrangement. Decide on a time when you're going to get physical and then do all you can to get yourself in the mood, such as a bath, delicious food, candles or a chat. Enjoy each other.

Don't expect mind-bending lust – mildly being up for it is good enough. If it's been a long time and you're a bit nervous about having sex, go back to basics. It doesn't matter what you do as long as you're physically close. Being physically close without having penetrative sex can eventually kick start your libido. In fact, when you've been together for a while, you often need physical proximity to *start* feeling desire. In other words, you can' t hang around waiting for an overwhelming wave of lust to wash over you or you'll wait a long time. Start having sex and let Mother Nature take her course.

The bottom line is, if you can't be bothered to do all you can to get yourself and your partner in the mood for sex then you're a rotten lover. What's loving about a person who doesn't at least try? This is brutal, but it's true. Perhaps you're right to take your lover's constancy for granted even when you're not putting out, trusting that they'll stick by you. But they're almost certain to get depressed and unconfident – both traits are hell to live with and unlikely to endear them to you. Keeping your sex life extant is as important for your mental health as theirs.

9. Search for the hero

We know the score. You fell in love with a hero and now your relationship isn't as wonderful as when you first met. We'll help you track down your partner's lost appeal.

Do you miss the good old days, when your lover listened spellbound to your stories, treated you like the sexiest creature on earth and made you feel warm and fuzzy?

Have you heard that after the initial glow of romance, you're left with something deeper, more mature, that's, well, a bit boring really? That, once you've settled with your mate, spontaneity, romance and heroics are just for high days and holidays? It's just not true.

Of course relationships change with time. As we get to know our partners better, we often love them more deeply and feel a closer bond. But this new companionship should be an add-on to the old intensity, not an instead-of. In the drudgery of our daily grind, it's often far easier to look for problems than solutions. At times it might feel as if the hero or heroine you fell in love with has sneaked off, leaving behind a dull git or crone. We believe the hero is still there, waiting in the wings to be rediscovered and nurtured back to health.

It takes a bit of effort to root out your partner's inner hero and you might have to look quite hard. We know that when you're in a rut of

Here's an idea for you...

Time for a little live experiment. Spend a day noticing and appreciating all your partner's mini heroics. Try to make at least twelve comments, like: 'I love the way that even though you've been up half the night with the baby, you still look gorgeous.' At the end of the day, spend a little time alone evaluating your partner's responses. We hope you're pleasantly surprised.

working, shopping, cooking, bringing up kids, cleaning, watching television, arguing and worrying, it can be hard to believe there's a hero inside your tired, sniping partner. If that sounds familiar, we suggest you ring-fence half an hour to yourself, grab a sheet of paper and answers the following questions:

❀ Why do I love my partner?
❀ What would I miss if we weren't together?

The tricky part is to then share your answers with your partner. Instead of attaching your list to the fridge, sneak your responses into conversations. For example, if you love your partner's sense of humour, instead of just guffawing at her jokes, try making a comment like, 'I like it when you make me laugh. Nobody makes me laugh like you do.' Or, if you appreciate hubby getting your kids to stick to bedtime, say something like, 'I love the way you're a really hands-on dad. I couldn't have got the kids to bed without your help.'

Peel off the label

Everyone, your partner included, lives up or down to others' expectations. Try to avoid labelling your partner. If you think 'he's not romantic' or 'she's always late', you're less likely to notice the times when he does buy roses or when she arrives ahead of you.

If your girlfriend usually leaves you to do the laundry but one day does the ironing on a whim, resist the temptation to make a sarcastic comment like 'Are we expecting the Queen round for tea?' and instead try 'I really like it when you iron the shirts' (and don't tell her she's missed a bit).

Defining idea...

'I remember a lovely New Yorker cartoon, so poignant I cried. The drawing was of an obviously poor, overweight and exhausted couple sitting at their kitchen table. The husband, in his t-shirt, had not shaved. The wife had curlers in her hair. Dirty dishes and nappies hung on a makeshift clothesline strung from a pipe to the fridge. They were drinking coffee out of chipped old mugs. The caption was the man smiling at his wife, saying, "I just love the way you wrinkle your nose when you laugh".'

LEIL LOWNDES, relationship expert and author

Nobody can be a knight in shining armour every day, so as well as noticing the big stuff, show appreciation for small acts of kindness. Say your partner put off hanging a picture you were both given months ago. You come home one day and notice it up. Most of us would instinctively say something along the lines of 'I'm glad that picture is finally up'. The problem with that sort of comment is that it stresses the negative and sends your partner the message that he's a bit of a procrastinator. Hardly heroic. But if you breeze in and exclaim, 'Oh that looks fantastic. I really like the way you've hung that', he'll feel like a hero inside and be more likely to act like one. It's crucial to watch your tone as well as your turn of phrase, so that you sound more like an impressed temptress than a disappointed schoolmistress.

10. Take your love outside

Walking is wonderful. Need to clear your heads of clutter and put problems into proper perspective? Take a hike. Chances are you'll walk out with a problem and home with a solution.

Whether you saunter in companionable silence or amble in animated conversation, nothing quite matches a daily constitutional. It's an escape from domesticity and a chance to reconnect with the person who matters.

Let's be pedestrian

Unless you live in an offshore lighthouse, there is always somewhere to walk. The sort of journey we're talking about does not need to have a specific purpose or destination, though it might involve the collection of a newspaper or be broken up by a pint in a local pub; the real reason is to have a change of environment and a change of air. Open spaces have mind-expanding properties which help you to think more clearly; all of a sudden, difficulties become more doable and problems less problematic. Walking boosts your level of serotonin, the feel-good chemical in our brains. It also releases the body's natural opiates, endorphins, giving you a buzz. When we walk with our partners we associate feeling high with him or her.

Here's an idea for you...

Next time you find yourself getting into an argument, why not suggest you go for a walk together to take time out and regain your composure? You might agree not to discuss the contested subject, or do so only after an interval of, say, half an hour.

As we know all too well, small spaces can be constricting and close down creative processes. Try to walk every day, or at least a couple of times a week. Whether you live in the city or the country there will be something to explore, so try to take new routes every time rather than just going on the same journey every day. In the countryside, by the sea, in every village and town there is always something to see, hear, touch and feel. Life is different on foot, the pace is slower, there are fewer distractions and you don't have to worry about parking, drink driving or one-way streets.

Marching orders

If one of you feels like walking out, go for a walk together. Walks give couples a chance to talk and think. And on warm summer evenings a chance to stop and drink. And it goes without saying that a walk will make any meal eaten afterwards all the more enjoyable.

Memory lane

Walking can perk up your relationship in different ways. Perhaps, like many couples, you went for more walks in your 'courting days'. Going for walks, years or even decades into a relationship, may take you not only down Pineview Avenue, but down memory lane as well. Indeed, if you make the same journey, retracing forgotten steps, those old passionate feelings will probably return.

Defining idea...

'Where'er you walk, cool gales shall fan the glade. Trees where you tread, the blushing flow'rs shall rise. And all things flourish where you turn your eyes.'

ALEXANDER POPE

Two's company, three or more is a rambling association

Many couples find that joining a walking club gives them a sharper focus and opportunities to meet like-minded saunterers or strollers. If there isn't a club within a short walking distance from your home, why not start one?

But if asked for a definitive reason for endorsing walks, one word comes to mind: serendipity – the faculty of making happy and unexpected accidental discoveries. Sometimes it is what we discover in the environment: a new building site to spy on, a skip to raid, an unexpectedly lovely garden, a mis-spelt ad in a shop window. More often, the happy discovery is something one of us says, triggered by something we have seen. A walk is a journey into your partner's head and heart.

Defining idea...

'I like long walks, especially when they are taken by people who annoy me.'

FRED A. ALLEN, American radio comic

11. Sorry seems to be the hardest word

Some of us would rather face a firing squad than admit we're wrong. If the 's' word sticks in your throat, it's time to bite the bullet.

Everyone screws up sometimes. We all make mistakes, forget important dates and break promises. But trying to blame your partner makes them feel bad and drags them down to the same level.

The trouble is, deep down you both know you've messed up, and it mangles trust. How do we know? Been there, done that and learnt the hard way that owning up and apologising helps rebuild damaged trust between lovers.

'I'm sorry.' Sounds simple doesn't it? But why do so many of us struggle to say it? Perhaps you are afraid of losing face or looking weak. After all, saying sorry means admitting you're wrong. Perhaps you feel resentful because you always end up apologising first. It could be that it's not your fault or you don't see eye to eye. It's hard to say sorry when you don't know why your partner is angry or upset. Maybe your partner made sarcastic comments when you tried to apologise last time or won't accept your apology, so you wonder what the point is.

Here's an idea for you...

Try saying sorry next time you catch yourself hurting your partner's feelings. In your mind, rate how difficult it was out of ten, where ten is 'will the ground please open and swallow me up'. Your first couple of apologies might feel off the scale, but once you've had a bit of practice, you'll get it down to an easier two or three.

When to say sorry

The best time to say sorry is as soon as you notice that you've hurt your partner. Now, we're not saints either, and know it's incredibly difficult to break mid-argument and offer an apology. Especially if you're winning. If you can express regret after, or even during, an argument, great. On the other hand, it's often preferable to calm down a bit so you don't sound sarcastic or insincere.

How to say sorry

Saying sorry is useless unless your partner knows why you're apologising. You need to acknowledge what you've done wrong. Be specific. It might make you squirm, but which of these apologies packs most punch?

'I'm sorry.'
'I'm sorry you're upset.'
'I'm sorry I upset you by calling you a lazy slag. I didn't mean it. I came home irritable and took it out on you. I know I shouldn't have said it.'

Sarcasm or a half-hearted apology, like 'You know I didn't mean it' or 'You know I'm not all bad', is worse than no apology at all because your partner will probably feel you are being disingenuous.

Defining idea…

'You're either part of the problem or you're part of the solution.'
ELDRIDGE CLEAVER, founder of the Black Panthers

How to accept an apology

Apologies need to be accepted with grace and good will, rather than as ammunition for mud slinging and accusation. 'Ha! I knew it was all your fault, you horrid little worm, and now you've accepted it' is a great way not to accept an apology. There are millions of variations of it, but you usually know when you are not accepting an apology properly, as there's only really one right way: 'Thank you.' So if it's tempting to gloat, remember: you'll probably need to say sorry for something soon yourself.

More than words…

Words are sometimes enough, but actions usually speak louder. This doesn't mean proffering a potted cheese plant or box of peppermint creams every time you feel an

Defining idea…

'Everyone makes mistakes. To forgive those mistakes is an action of love.'
JOHN GRAY, author of *Men are from Mars, Women are from Venus*

apology coming on. Gifts can make your partner feel pressurised or even blackmailed into accepting your apology before he's ready. If you can't resist saying it with flowers, make sure this isn't the only time you buy your beloved blooms. Far better to follow your verbal apology with action related to your transgression. If your partner's cross because you never wash up, get the rubber gloves on or buy a dishwasher. If your girlfriend's upset after finding your stash of *Horny Housewife*, cancel the subscription. Whatever you've done, there's no greater crime than apologising only to commit the same sin again. If you've wounded with words rather than with deeds, action is still called for. When you've said sorry, hold out your hand. Invite your partner to come to you, not to lunge at you.

12. The biggest turn off

Looking for a quick fix for a dwindling relationship? This one's fast, free and fantastically simple. Unplug your telly and plug in to an amazing life together.

When did you last watch something on TV that transformed your relationship for the better? Time for some home truths: it's big, it's ugly and it rots relationships.

Not tonight, Joseph

Are you sick of your partner hogging the remote control? Do you continually fall asleep over soaps, reality shows or celebrity snowboarding? Most of us recognise the damaging effect that television has on our children, but what about our love lives? We think the hold television has on society is scary. Yet the role it plays in people's lives is rarely questioned. Decades ago, broadcasts only took place in the evenings and weekend afternoons. The service closed down at midnight and what telly there was, was watched on one machine in a communal area by whole families. Not any more. The telly is taking up more and more of lovers' free time and energy. Most couples watch around four hours of television a day. Television, like a baby cuckoo, insidiously pushes everything else out of the love nest. And at what cost? Is that manic machine in the corner interrupting your conversations,

Here's an idea for you...

Getting rid of the telly seems too radical? Why not have a telly-free month? Put the box, or boxes, in the attic tonight and in four weeks time see how you've got on. Both keep a journal of your thoughts and feelings, and write down how you spent all that time.

preventing candlelit dinners or maybe even stopping you trying out other ideas in this book? Whether you're channel hopping, station surfing or really engrossed in episode 307 of that sexy sitcom, you're missing four hours a day of prime time real life.

Unplug the box and plug into a wonderful life

When we tell people we haven't got a television, they think we're eccentric, mad or seriously weird. Usually they wink and ask us what we do in our evenings. We do a lot: mooch around markets, cruise on the river, see old movies on the big screen, snoop about in galleries, visit exhibitions, comedy clubs, musicals, quirky fringe plays and a lot of other fun stuff. We're not joined at the hip and use our bonus four hours to do lots of things on our own or with other friends.

Defining idea...

'Television? The word is half Greek, half Latin. No good can come out of it.'
C.P. SCOTT, legendary editor of the
Manchester Guardian

Take up a sport, join a book club, learn a language or develop your artistic side. We're not saying you need to do all of these things, or any of them – you need to choose the activities that would suit you. How could you recharge your relationship in a few extra hours a day? Maybe you'd like to have time to go running together, make your partner a sculpture, become part-time puppeteers or join the local choir. Flick the off switch, get your life back and your relationship will prosper. Whatever you do, it's better than being passive voyeurs of other peoples' lives.

Defining idea...

'Television displaces other romantic opportunities. Like brushing up against your wife's backside in the kitchen. The old fashioned challenge of having to entertain each other.'

JIM PETERSEN, author of *Playboy's History of the Sexual Revolution*

13. The least you need to do...

...to keep your relationship minty fresh.

Read, digest and ponder. Then get your diary, a big red pen and start prioritising your relationship.

This chapter contains the three golden rules of a healthy relationship – the *sine qua non* of sexual happiness. All the technique and creativity in the world isn't going to fix the sex in a relationship where the couple is together but not *together*. On the other hand, couples that spend time together, and anticipate and plan for those times, find it hard to lose interest in one another.

Rule 1: Daily...

How is your partner feeling right now? What's happening at work? How are their relationships with friends, colleagues, siblings, parents? Carve out fifteen minutes of every day to talk. If you find yourselves getting into a rut of busyness, when you pass like ships in the night for several days in a row without touching base, either go to bed before your usual time or get up earlier and have a coffee together so you can touch base.

Kiss each other every morning before you get out of bed. Take the time for a swift cuddle. Breathe deeply. Hold tight. Do the same at night. Never take your physical intimacy for granted. In this Vale of Tears we

Here's an idea for you...

Look for easy ways to cheer your partner up. Pick up a tub of her favourite ice-cream on the way home from work. Run him a bath and bring him a beer. Sappy gestures work – they build up a huge bank of goodwill that couples can draw on when life gets stressful.

call life, you found each other. Pretty amazing. Worth acknowledging that with at least a daily hug, methinks.

Rule 2: Weekly...

Go out with each other once a week where humanly possible. Once a fortnight is the bare minimum. According to the experts, this is the most important thing you can do. Couples who keep dating, keep mating. Spending too long sloping around the same house does something to a couple's sexual interest in each other and what it does generally isn't good. So get out, preferably after making some small effort to tart yourself up so you're visually pleasing to your partner. Let them see why they bothered with you in the first place. (No, I never said this chapter was rocket science. I just said that it worked.)

Rule 3: Monthly...

Go for a mini-adventure – shared memories cement your relationship. Make your adventure as mad or staid as you like, but at the least make sure it's something that you haven't done since the beginning of your relationship. It really doesn't matter what it is, as long as it's not your usual 'date'.

What's the point? You see your partner coping with new environments and new skills and that keeps you interested in them. And them in you. Simple.

Defining idea...

'Good sex begins when your clothes are still on.'
MASTERS and JOHNSON, sex research pioneers

If you're shaking your head and tutting 'how banal', I'd get that smug look off your face, pronto. Research shows quite clearly that one of the defining differences between strong couples and 'drifting' couples is the amount of effort and time they spend on their shared pursuits. All of us have heard the advice, 'Spend more time with each other being as interesting as possible.' But how many couples do you know who actually do it? I'm prepared to bet that those who do seem happiest.

14. The love's there, but the lust's gone AWOL

Hey sexual pioneer! Yes, we're talking to you.

If you're a baby boomer in a sexual relationship that's lasted more than nine years, then you're breaking new sexual ground. The human race doesn't have much practice of doing what you're doing. We simply don't know how to do long-term relationships.

As Dr Alan Altman writes in *Making Love the Way We Used To, Or Better*, 'Many people are disappointed when they can't re-create those early thrilling feelings. [But] We don't really have many examples of how to keep a 25 plus year marriage alive sexually. At the turn of a century a 47-year-old male was considered old.'

Are we programmed to get bored with a long-term partner? There's a persuasive argument that we are. Psychologists believe that one reason we go off sex with long-term lovers is the powerful anti-incest taboos that are part of nearly every culture. Basically, in a 'functional' family, brothers and sisters who are brought up together don't fancy each other despite incredible proximity. However, brothers and sisters who are brought up apart often do. It may be that if we live too long with someone of the opposite sex, we stop reacting to their sexual charisma. This is why we must never get too cosy with each other or allow our boundaries to become too melded.

65

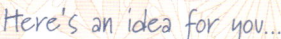

Here's an idea for you...

A long-term sexual relationship will go in cycles – sometimes strong, sometimes fading. Sexual desire is something you can rekindle, but make sure your partner is singing from the same hymn sheet. When the first flush of lust passes, it won't come back without will and compassion from each of you for the other.

We long for the thrills of the beginning of the relationship. We yearn for the time when our partners were mad for us. Sometimes we want it so much that we move onto another relationship to get the kicks. So there's the bad news. Your challenge is to decide what to do about it. Interview the sexual pioneers – women and men who have successfully lived with each other for many years – and they talk touchingly about the power that sexuality shared with one partner over many years can hold. One woman interviewed by writer Brigid McConville in her book *The Secret Life* says, 'We have been together for so long, when I look at him not just as my ageing bloke but as the man who made love to me on the beach in Greece, on the train across Europe, and tied to the bedposts in a hotel in Spain. No one else has those intimate memories, just us. No one else knows what he is capable of. It's a bond so strong it's a bit like having children together: nothing can change the history of our intimacy and what we have made and shared and I can conjure up images of us making love together any time I like.'

How do you get to the place where a lifetime's worth of loving experience informs your view of your lover? In a nutshell: don't get boring and don't get bored. Ask yourself some hard questions. If you love your partner but are no longer excited by them, reverse it. How exciting are you? How passionate are you? Would you fancy yourself? Do you feel alive?

Are you passionate about work or your interests? Do you have any interests?

Are you enthusiastic about your children, your friends and the things you talk about with them?

What projects do you have on the backburner for the future that excite you?

If you're drawing a blank here, it's time to get back your passion for life. There's absolutely no way you'll get it back for your partner without it. And be warned, moving onto another partner in the hope of regaining your passion for life will work in the short term, but never in the long term. This isn't always the complete answer to the 'love but no lust' dilemma, but it's the first crucial step.

Defining idea...

'**Anyone who knows Dan Quayle knows that he would rather play golf than have sex any day.**'
MARILYN QUAYLE, responding to charges that her husband had an affair while on a golf holiday

15. Developing sexual mystique

Yes, it's possible. Even if you've shared a bathroom for years.

Last night I had a moment of despair. I walked by a pub where I overheard a man saying to his (male) companion, 'So go on then, have a guess. How many clear shots did Portugal have at goal?'

Admittedly even his mate looked bored, but I thought, 'Here I am, working at building more understanding between the sexes in my own small way. And it's a total waste of time. Men and women? Different species. What's the point?'

Then my natural Pollyanna spirit kicked in, 'Differences – you know what? They're a Good Thing. In fact, if you want to keep your love life hot, they're an Essential Thing. To carry on fancying your partner and to have them carrying on fancying you, you need a little distance between you, a little mystery, a little wildness in your soul.'

And if that doesn't come naturally, you need to work at it.

'Male and female are different,' says relationship counsellor Paula Hall. 'And we've known since the sixties that if a couple want a stable relationship, it's worth working at maintaining that difference. It's what keeps the electric buzz between them.' She points out that studies by

Here's an idea for you...

In a nutshell, make it a habit that one night a week you do your own thing, no matter how busy you are. Remember, spending too much time inside together is terrible for your love life.

psychologists have already picked up on the dangers of becoming too alike. 'We call it "enmeshment" when couples become too similar,' says Hall. 'It's been known for a long time that it can have a detrimental impact on sexual desire.'

You probably think it's cosy that you share the same interests, friends, hopes, dreams, taste in soft furnishings. So it is. Congratulations. You're terrific mates. And carry on regardless if you want a great relationship without particularly exciting, or indeed plentiful, sex. However, if you want sex that makes your toes curl, you need a little separateness to keep desire alive.

You can be all things to a partner, but not to a lover. They cannot be all things to you.

There's an art to this. One woman I interviewed made a point of always being just a little bit cool with her husband every three or four months or so. 'Nothing serious,' she said, 'I'd just switch off from him a bit. Seem a little bit less easily pleased. A bit more interested in talking to my friends on the phone. Lock myself in the bathroom. Submerge myself in a book. Really trivial stuff. Worked like a charm. Within a week, he'd be suggesting weekends away in Paris and voluntarily arranging babysitting so we could go out to dinner.' (NB I can't resist the opportunity here to remind men of the huge aphrodisiac potential in occasionally arranging a babysitter. In most relationships, whether or not the woman works from home or not, she does the babysitting stuff – it's so goddamn nice when your partner sorts it out for once as it's such a clear signal that you want to spend some time with her. Try it.)

Defining idea...

'An absence, the declining of an invitation to dinner, an unintentional, unconscious harshness are of more service than all the cosmetics and fine clothes in the world.'
MARCEL PROUST

All this withdrawing interest sounds suspiciously like game-playing – and you know what, it is! You can fake it a little bit like my interviewee, but it doesn't always work. What does always work is if both partners do it for real – keep interested in life, stay full of vim and brio for other projects, remain engaged with people outside of their relationship and be passionate about the world. Then, and here is the important bit, they bring that energy home and translate it into passion for each other. They do that by talking about their lives with such enthusiasm that their partners can't help get a kick out of their enthusiasm, charm, intelligence and all-round top-quality personality.

The least you need to do...

Relationship psychologist Susan Quilliam points out that there are straightforward ways of making sure your relationship doesn't sink into the mire of 'enmeshment'.

Rule 1. All couples fall into a pattern of doing the same thing and being scared to suggest anything new because 'we don't do that'. But if you fancy doing something different, suggest it anyway. Don't argue if they say 'no'. The point has been made. You've reinforced in both your minds that you're different individuals.

Rule 2. Support your partner as much as possible when they're trying to be an individual. Don't dismiss new ideas and interests without thinking them through carefully.

Rule 3. Be yourself. Don't take on his or her interests and hobbies unless they genuinely interest you, too. We're equal but we're not the same.

73

16. Should I stay or should I go?

Love life hit an iceberg? How do you know when to hang in there and salvage a wrecked relationship and when to swim for new shores?

Call us die-hard romantics, but we believe most relationships are salvageable. Even after betrayal, arguments, debt or months of sexual drought, it's possible to recapture the spark and ignite something rich and purposeful.

Even the best relationships feel like sinking ships sometimes, and the urge to escape with the nearest lifeboat man can be strong. But the decision about whether to stay in a lacklustre love affair or find a new port in the storm should be a rational one.

Resist making decisions on a whim. Even if you've caught your new groom in bed with your bridesmaid, stay put. Sometimes you'll find yourself changing your mind from day to day, or even hour to hour. In truth, many people who leave relationships impulsively later regret it, only to find it's too late to return. You've probably invested many months or years in your alliance. Parents, in-laws and friends will all give you their views, but it's not really any of their business. They've all got their own agenda, so we suggest you avoid discussing your dilemma until you've reached your decision.

Here's an idea for you...

When it's hard to decide whether to stay or go, it's usually because both options have a lot going for them. Whatever you decide, an informed choice is better than an impulsive one. When you have a moment, make a list of what first attracted you to your partner. What are his good qualities? What would you miss? In what ways does he bring out the best in you?

Write stuff

Writing your thoughts down brings clarity and helps you decide. Try keeping a diary of thoughts and feelings. What do you want from your relationship? Why do you feel like leaving? Is it your relationship that is making you unhappy or could there be other reasons, like a career crisis or mounting debts? If there has been a catastrophe, like infidelity, be honest with yourself about what your relationship was like before. Do you have something worth saving or were you thinking about leaving anyway? If your relationship was good before, you may well decide to give it another go. See if you can discover what your partner wants. Even if your problems seem insurmountable, good intentions on both sides go a long way. Can you see the difficulties as a catalyst for change?

What can you do if you are incompatible? Charlie wants six children, but Denise doesn't want any. Russell wants a pet tarantula and Sally's arachnophobic. Stephanie wants to live in a city, but Jo's a committed country dweller. George wants sex twice a day, Jenny would be happy with twice a year. As we said, we're die-hard romantics and think we can reconcile most so-called irreconcilable differences with goodwill, compromise and imagination. But romance alone won't do. It takes both of you to look at problems and come up with creative solutions. Charlie retrained as a childminder. Sally had her phobia treated and has grown rather fond of Gideon the tarantula. Stephanie and Jo live in a country-style cottage in a small commuter town. And Jenny and George? Don't be so nosy – that's their business!

Having said that, we've identified four relationship scenarios that are bad news. There's no point staying together if:

His pants are on fire

Persistent liars cause big trouble. Relationships are about trust. Can't believe a word he says? Get packing.

He's mad, bad and dangerous to know

Rachel's partner Damien was convinced she was having an affair. She wasn't. He hired a private detective to follow her and then accused her of bribing the detective to lie on her behalf. He went through her laundry, checking her knickers for semen stains. Every day when she came home he interrogated her about where she'd been. This sort of jealousy is rare and is a sign of illness, often related to hitting the bottle.

In the trade it's called Othello Syndrome. Rachel was advised to get out of the relationship, as there was a risk that Damien might kill her. If this sort of behaviour sounds at all familiar, get out and get expert help for your partner. You may be able to re-energise your relationship, but they need treatment first.

He subjects you to degrading treatment

If he persistently puts you down in public or humiliates you in front of your friends, don't stand for it. Nobody deserves to have her self worth eroded by an insecure gronk who helps themselves to feel better by making their lovers look stupid, useless or inept.

He's hitting home

You can't salvage your relationship if your partner is threatening, hitting or sexually assaulting you. Domestic violence happens in every sort of relationship, and is hardly ever a one-off. Sometimes it's there from the start; sometimes it won't surface for years. Lots of people stay because they are frightened, or hope things will improve. But it usually gets worse over time. Get out and get help from the police, doctor or local helpline.

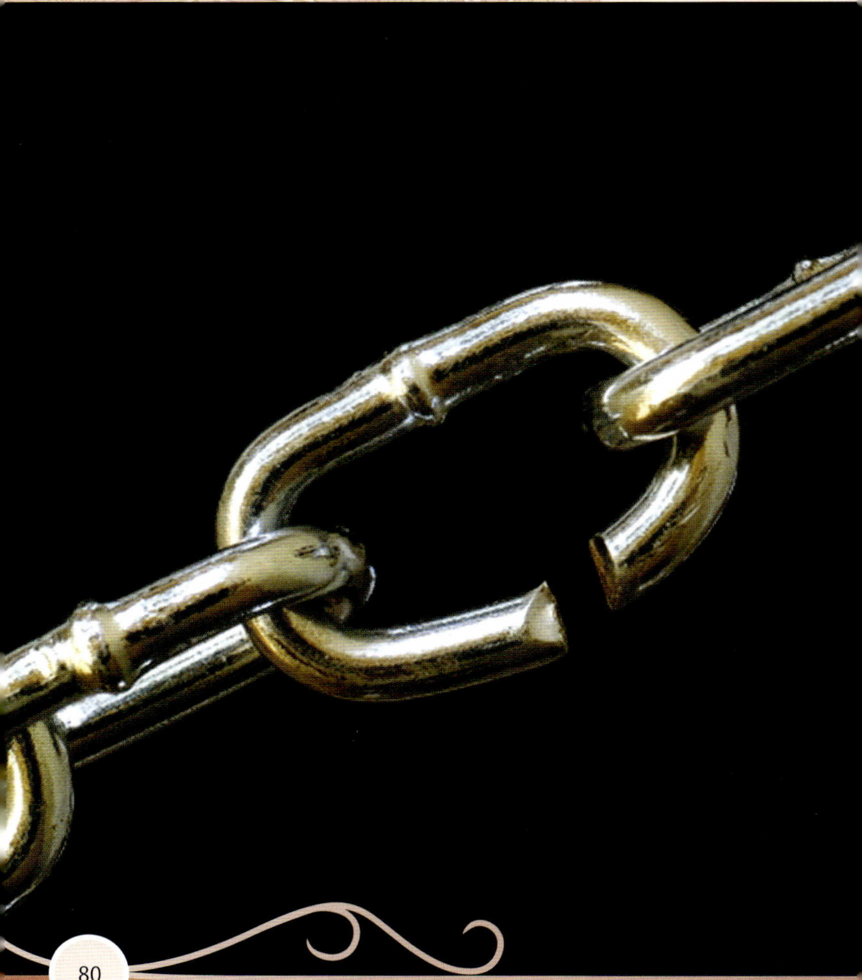

17. Breaking up is hard to do – but sometimes, you have to

Sometimes it just isn't there. You have pushed, prodded and tried to shoehorn this person into a relationship, but it just isn't going to work.

So you need to grab the bull by the horns (or rather let go of it) and move on. And there is a right and a wrong way to do it.

Getting it right lets both of you move on with dignity and calm, but getting it wrong can leave you both licking your wounds and making voodoo dolls for months, if not years, to come.

How to split up with a good one

Oh, if only it was possible to flip the X factor like a light switch. Sometimes it just doesn't work and you've got to cut a nice guy loose. The best way to deal with men like this is face to face and showing them the respect they deserve, even if it makes things a little harder for you. That way they, and you, can rest assured that you did the dignified thing. But once you are sitting opposite, what do you say?

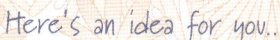

Here's an idea for you...

If you think a break-up may turn ugly, do it in a public place and have a friend come and meet you at a prearranged time. That way, you are making a clear statement that the meeting is over.

✿ Don't lie. Making up a dead aunt or work stress is unfair. If they have done right by you don't slope off under the cover of a fib; they will probably be able to tell and worry about what else you have lied to them about.

✿ Be as honest as you can be. If the spark is just missing, tell them that. It's not uncommon for lots of things to be right but one thing to be wrong and you can even commiserate with them; chances are if you aren't feeling it, they won't be either.

✿ Don't suggest it might happen further down the line. If they really like you they will keep hanging in there waiting for you to change your mind, which is stopping them from finding someone else. No matter how reassuring for you it would be to have a nice guy waiting in the wings in case you don't find Mr Right, it's wrong, wrong, wrong…

✿ Answer any questions with the best framing possible. When people are upset they may level a lot of hurt questions at you; try not to respond in kind. If they ask if it was because you didn't like their knobbly chicken legs, don't start clucking. You can simply say you didn't feel a sexual chemistry; after all, one woman's chicken legs are another woman's lean, athletic pins. There is no point in dashing his confidence. At the same time, if his fifteen phone calls a day did irritate you, you could let him know. It might stop him from making the same mistake again.

Defining idea...

'Saying goodbye doesn't mean anything. It's the time we spent together that matters, not how we left it.'
TREY PARKER and MATT STONE, creators of South Park, the US cartoon show

✿ Balance criticism with positivity. If you are going to mention the fifteen calls a day, then make sure that you let him know that while being attentive was great, it could be moderated (not stopped). You don't want to release him onto an unsuspecting female population imagining that the best way to take things forward is never to pick up the phone.

✿ Don't use them for ex sex. What for you is just a convenient lay, might keep their hurt alive and erode their confidence, whilst fostering false hope.

✿ Don't tell them how they feel. You have had time to get used to the idea; it's news to them and they may feel disappointed or that you had more potential.

✿ Stick to your guns. Just because they think you still have something between you if you really haven't, keep reminding them that you don't think that it's the case. You will only have to go through this again further down the line. And do you really want people lying in bed at night trying to interpret what you said? Heartless!

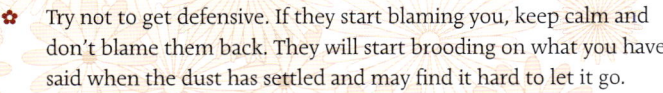

❀ Try not to get defensive. If they start blaming you, keep calm and don't blame them back. They will start brooding on what you have said when the dust has settled and may find it hard to let it go.

How to split up with a bad one

Well, I'm showing my dark side here, but who cares? If someone has been mean or destructive towards you, they are not entitled to any respect in return. The problem is that sometimes our judgement gets a little bit clouded. I suggest that if you aren't sure, just keep it short and sweet. If they are real meanies, and have left you hanging on for phone calls/stood you up/left you dying of thirst in a desert, try some of the silent treatment back. A few days in dating no-man's-land waiting for the phone to ring might teach these men a few lessons about empathy. And if they hate you for it, who cares? Save your good stuff for those who deserve it.

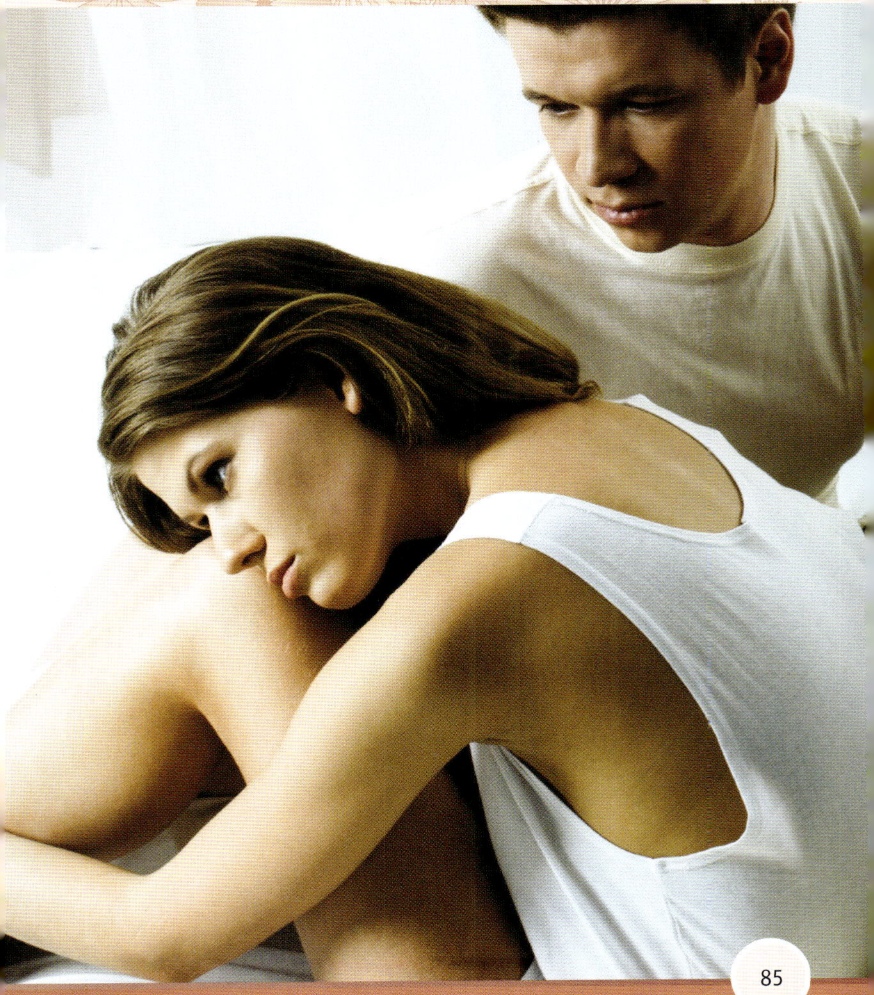

18. Getting over rejection

Along with the highs and the fun of dating, comes some of the rough stuff.

That's to be expected, but it doesn't make it any easier when someone says, 'thanks, but no thanks'.

The key to enjoying dating is to accept that just as everyone you meet can't light your fire, you're not everyone's idea of petrol either. But that's all very well in theory. You need some practical tools to make sure that you can stay afloat when buffeted by romance's vagaries.

Smile, smile, smile!

When someone wants to make a break, let them go. Even if you think someone is making a mistake and there is potential in your relationship, no one normally wants to be anyone else's jailer. By all means, ask some questions if you think it will help, but don't plead, beg or whine. You'll be glad you kept your dignity when the initial discomfort has paled. Help is at hand…

✿   Where is it coming from? You've only had three dates and you feel like you will never get over the rejection? This guy probably isn't the reason; hell, you don't even know this guy. You may just have some old feelings that are coming up to do with your own

Here's an idea for you...

If you are finding it hard to get over the knock to your confidence, try going somewhere where taking risks is all part of some good harmless fun. Speed-dating is a good way to see that this is all just a numbers game, to some degree; your right number just hasn't come up yet.

confidence; a man shouldn't have this much effect so early on; you may need to look more closely at your own demons. You may also worry that he was your last shot at children, a home, someone to strut down the aisle with. This is just fear talking. Relax, you will get another shot at fulfilling your dreams.

❀ Letting go of control. You might think that if you had tried a different technique, worn different clothes or could just have one more chat with him you could turn things around. You can't. The great thing about being in a relationship is that two willing people choose it; once you can accept that you can't control everything, you can enjoy the fact that you aren't responsible for everything either.

❀ Get back in the swing. If someone wanted to end a brief fling, catching a glimpse of you sloping round the supermarket in your pyjamas will just reaffirm their conviction. It also means that the fantastically handsome guy fumbling through the meals for one is only going to speak to you to ask you where the air fresheners are. Even if you don't feel perky, act it: before you know it, the balance will be less act and more reality.

❀ What were you expecting? Something to do every Saturday night? Someone to rely on? Maybe you need to get a life that doesn't revolve around someone else and theirs. You will be much more likely to take rejection and break-ups more easily if your whole social structure isn't hinged around the other person.

✿ Don't put words in his mouth. Don't imagine that you know what he is thinking. You don't know whether he wants to get back with his ex or try naked wrestling with his best friend Stuart. The point is, he doesn't want you and the worst kind of guy you can try and get involved with is one that doesn't really want you. You could get arrested for it, but worse, you could spend pointless months, years even, staring at the ceiling in the small hours of the morning trying to work out what went wrong when he doesn't even remember your name.

✿ Get the chocolate out. Get the duvet on the sofa, have a good sob, drink a glass of wine and eat some chocolate all the while berating this fool that can't see what a prize you are to your most supportive mate. A knock to the confidence deserves a little ego stroke. Then get up tomorrow and move on.

And finally, remind yourself what this is about. Dating in itself is not a solution to all your problems, but then neither should a man be. Remind yourself that you are meant to be having fun and taking a few risks. Then put on your best outfit and hit the dance floor again.

Re-energise your sex life

Are you sensual?

How many of the following have you done in the last two weeks?

- ■ Massaged your skin with scented lotion or oils.
- ■ Walked into a room thinking, 'God, I look hot'.
- ■ Slipped on a pair of heels just to admire how they make your legs and feet look.
- ■ Bathed by candlelight.
- ■ Flirted with a stranger.
- ■ Got totally caught up listening to a song that makes you feel 10 years younger.
- ■ Made the first move.
- ■ Exposed your body to a fabric that feels sensuous.
- ■ Danced in the rain.
- ■ Danced anywhere.
- ■ Watched a sunset or sunrise.
- ■ Eaten too much 'bad' food, drunk too much good wine.
- ■ Got into bed naked.
- ■ Contemplated buying a sex toy.
- ■ Laughed so hard, you probably didn't look pretty.
- ■ Bought a beauty product that you didn't really need.
- ■ Read or written erotic fiction.
- ■ Said 'I love you' and really meant it.
- ■ Said 'I want you' and really meant it.
- ■ Had a thundering orgasm.

19. Be contrary

Put your love life in reverse gear. If you avoid sex, chase it. If there's a position you love, don't do it. Courting frustration could be just the trip you need to drive you over the edge.

Being intimate is a double-edged sword. Sometimes it brings you too close and you need to be a bit more sexually ruthless to enjoy getting off. Over time it's almost inevitable for a couple's sex life to decrease in frequency. Often we're simply unrealistic about our sexual expectations because our culture is saturated with images of sex and romantic longing. We feel like we should want more, and this unfocused yearning can lead to people seeking out affairs. It's possible to be in an endless cycle of falling in love, getting disillusioned, meeting someone else and repeating the whole cycle; Elizabeth Taylor once described herself as 'addicted to love'.

In reality the thing we have to deal with most when we grapple with sexual problems is our own psyche. During sex we have to open ourselves up to our vulnerabilities. Psychotherapist Dr Michael Bader says in Arousal: The Secret Logic of Sexual Fantasies: 'We go to bed naked in more ways than one.' We all carry insecurities with us that have been with us from childhood, and at first a new sexual liaison gives us a chance to work against this. If a woman has grown up feeling physically inferior to her beautiful mother, she might initially take

Here's an idea for you...

Ask your partner to describe your contribution to your lovemaking; make a careful note of what he says, then for a limited time reverse this behaviour. If he normally initiates sex, you do it for a change. You'll have sex sessions using completely different methods and techniques to the ones you're used to, and perhaps you'll be pleasantly surprised!

refuge in a relationship with an especially attractive man. However, over time, her old insecurities will emerge and return to plague her, and this is why so many couples start to experience sexual problems after the 'honeymoon period' which were not at first apparent.

Some couples say they have less sex but it's more intimate; however, this has its own problems. The more intimate you become, the more you're aware of your partner's frailties. Dr Bader also says: 'As couples get to know each other, their deeper awareness of each other's vulnerabilities can become their undoing. The other's inhibitions and the shame upon which they rest begin to wear down spontaneity and passion. We are just too close, too identified with our inhibited partner, to escape the experience.' It's important for you to have a certain degree of sexual ruthlessness and sometimes we all need some kind of emotional distance (via fantasy or physical space) in order to be able to switch off and concentrate on our own sexual needs.

If your sex life is nothing to write home about, try deliberately avoiding it for a while. If something's on tap you take it for granted. See how long you can go without having sex together. It's a good idea not to stop all physical activity: you could try masturbating separately and telling each other all about it when you do get together. The idea is to get you hot, but you can still agree whether to postpone sex or not – and maybe tomorrow when you eventually succumb to passion it'll be even better. Sometimes being frustrated, that feeling of suppressed longing, leads to the best sex of all so it's worth waiting until you just can't hold back.

To objectify your partner a little, you could also try playing around with sexual fantasy. Get him to dress up a little differently or speak to you in bed in a different voice. You're trying to think of him erotically as a means to give you great sex, rather than your soulmate with lots of problems he wants to talk over.

Over time we can desexualise our partners, so now's the time to inject some throbbing desire into the proceedings. It could be that he's treating you gently when you really want to be ravaged, so try talking dirty and see if this makes it easier for you to get excited. Force yourself to expose your throbbing desires. That's it – get low and dirty and sex up your relationship.

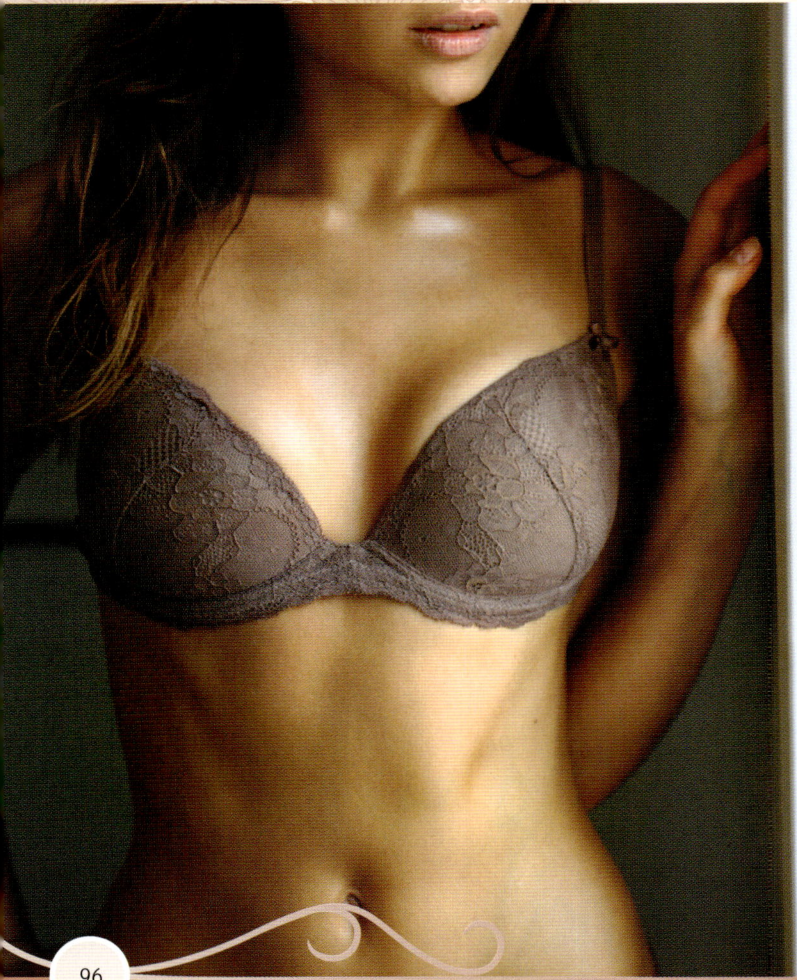

20. The power of lovely lingerie

Underwear. It's crucial. Get it right and you feel great. It's an essential part of being incredibly sexy.

It boosts your confidence and helps you look marvellous in and out of your clothes. What's not to love?

When I first travelled to the continent I was amazed at all the little underwear shops selling smalls at what I thought were extortionate prices. I reasoned that there was nothing wrong with a pack of five knickers for the price of one bra-strap in some chichi shop. Up to a point I was right. There are days when those cotton no-frills knickers work well. But what is truly different about your average French woman, is that she will wear sexy matching bra and knickers every day. And she is prepared to spend around £60 on each ensemble.

Now that I live in France I have gone very French in my attitude towards underwear. My bra and knicker drawers are stuffed full of matching ensembles. And oddly enough, once I started on this gig, I found it hard to go back to the five-packs. There's something empowering about matching top and bottom and for this reason you should seriously consider buying at least two pairs of knickers with each bra. To make sure you don't suffer from the dreaded VPL under trousers always make at least one of these pairs a g-string, or try out French knickers or boxer shorts for girls – no VPL and damn sexy!

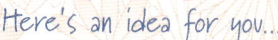

Here's an idea for you...

This expensive underwear is all very well, but a pain to hand wash. I take mine into the shower with me and wash it there, which is much easier. It also means you don't end up with that awful grey shade of white as your smalls get washed on a 60 degree cycle with all the wrong colours. Treat it well, and it will last much longer.

Sex appeal has a lot to do with confidence and there is nothing like good underwear to enhance your body shape and make you feel more attractive. For the flatter-chested among us, there is no more comforting moment than pulling a T-shirt over a new Wonderbra and seeing our body shapes totally transformed. For larger ladies, a good well-fitting bra is even more essential. If you want to minimise your bust under business suits, get measured by an expert to find out your correct cup size – you will lose 10lbs, I swear, immediately you put on the right fitting bra. And if you want to emphasise your cleavage, a right fitting bra does this stupendously well, besides being much more comfortable.

A sexy g-string can work wonders for your buttocks. Some people find them incredibly uncomfortable – I did to begin with – but once you get used to them you will hardly ever wear ordinary knickers again.

If you're wearing the right underwear, you feel like you can take on the world.

It makes you feel so much more confident. You walk into a business meeting and although the others can't see what you've got on underneath your suit, you know, and it gives you a sense of superiority. I spoke to Chantal Thomass, France's leading underwear designer, on this subject. 'Lingerie is fundamental to the way a woman feels,' she says, 'if your underwear isn't right, nothing else works.' A friend of mine says it determines her whole mood for the day: 'It's the first thing I put on and it puts me in a good or bad mood,' she says. 'I have a very intimate relationship with my lingerie, after all it is the thing I put on next to my skin.'

As we all know, for whatever reason, men adore stockings and suspenders. Just about every man I know is totally gone on them. 'I don't know what it is about them,' says one. 'They just drive me wild. Maybe it's because all the Playboy models I lusted over in my youth wore them.' Our job here is not to analyse, just wear them. Classic black suspender belts are the best but red can be good for a special occasion, adding an extra sex-vixen allure. The great thing about kinky or sexy underwear is that it enhances your sex drive as well as your partner's. You're hardly going to sit around feeling like a drudge in a pair of red crotchless knickers!

Defining idea…

'A lady is one who never shows her underwear unintentionally.'
LILLIAN DAY, American author

21. Enduring allure

It's not difficult to feel sexy at the beginning of a relationship. That first kiss is one of the most memorable things ever. Just the touch of your lover's hand will give you goose bumps.

But that sort of intensity doesn't last forever. Sadly it goes with time and with familiarity. What can you do to rekindle it?

I once read a story about a couple who had been together for years and got bored with one another. One night they both went to a party. For some reason she ended up naked in the host's bedroom. The lights were out, he came in and got into bed with her. They had fabulous sex and each only realised afterwards that they had slept with their spouse. Slightly far-fetched but what it highlights is the fact that great sex needn't stop. It's all in the mind. These people hadn't had sex with each other for months. Because each thought he or she was with someone else, that it was forbidden, they had a great time.

So, you need to get the fact that you are an old boring married couple out of your mind and start thinking about all the things that drove you wild about each other. You are still the same people, if a little older and more familiar – you just need to rediscover each other.

Here's an idea for you...

One evening sit down and reminisce. Go through your first date, what you wore, what you did, where you had sex. Talk about all the things that first attracted you to each other. Was it the way he talked, something he said? Was it a certain skirt she wore, the way she flicked her hair? This should bring back happy memories and rekindle lustful thoughts.

If you are married or living with someone and have children, finding the time to rediscover each other is not always easy. If you possibly can then go away together alone at least once every three months or so. It's not just the fact of being alone that's important, it's being away from all the chores and worries of home. It's hard to feel sexy when all you can talk about is a burst pipe, ill children and unpaid bills. You work all day, run the house, and collapse into bed exhausted at night. Not much time for sex. Try to think of sex as a priority and make time for it. Forget washing up, ironing or watching hours of television in the evening: slip into some sexy underwear and seduce your husband instead. What could be more important than that?

There are lots of little ways to make your everyday life sexier. Try to add spark to your life by thinking of each day as a day filled with sexy opportunities. Broaden your horizons: for example, don't just think of the bathroom as a place to shave but a place to rekindle your romance.

Being sexy is of course not just about looking good. Some friends of mine recently got divorced. The husband is a workaholic with his own business while the wife didn't work. 'I just lost respect for her,' he told me. 'I couldn't bear to see her wasting time and achieving nothing. She seemed to have no ambition whatsoever, no respect for herself or her own status. In the end she also had nothing to talk about, apart from what to eat or what the kids had done at school.' He sounds harsh but I see his point. He didn't care that his wife didn't work, but he did care that she never used her mind. There are those among us who want nothing more than the luxury of staying at home and raising our children, which is great as long as you don't forget that when you got married you were an interesting person in your own right and you need to ensure you stay that way.

Defining idea...

'Some people ask the secret of our long marriage. We take time to go to a restaurant two times a week. A little candlelit dinner, music and dancing. She goes Tuesdays, I go Fridays.'

HENRY YOUNGMAN, American comedian

22. Spice up your life

Time to reinvigorate yourself with something completely different.

You have already taken an important first step by buying this book. It is jam-packed full of tips on how to improve your sexiness and life. Another major step is to make routine a thing of the past.

Think differently to the pack. Be your own person and do your own thing. I'm not suggesting you go awol, but I am suggesting you use a little imagination to spice up your everyday life and increase your sexy image. Be more aware of your surroundings, look for the positive in the humdrum and create sexy situations where you normally wouldn't.

For example, your alarm goes off at 7am, you get up, have a shower, eat something, trudge down to the underground or the train in the pouring rain and go to work. This happens most days. However, some days, something different will break the monotony: a busker playing your favourite song, a story in the newspaper that makes you laugh, a brief glance from a fellow-commuter that sets something off in the depths of your half-asleep psyche. But to notice these things you have to be receptive and ready for them.

Here's an idea for you...

Surprise him by offering to wash his car, wearing a short skirt and stockings and suspenders. The neighbours will be eternally grateful too. Use your imagination to surprise people, including yourself!

Try to treat each day as an adventure. It's a terrible old cliché but live each day as if it were your last. Realistically you can't do that or you would never go to work but you get my drift? Instead of thinking 'God this is dreadful, I hate this commute' think 'I wonder what or who is waiting around the corner' or even if you're not so optimistic that anything remotely exciting awaits you on the 7.47 take something exciting with you like a novel full of steamy sex and adventure. Try reading Dangerous Liaisons or The Sexual Life of Catherine M on the train – it will at least get the imagination going of any commuter reading over your shoulder.

In terms of your sex life and your relationship, you should adopt the same approach. 'If there is a choice of what to do at the weekend, always go for the most eccentric one,' says a male friend of mine who has an above average success rate with members of the opposite sex. 'I find things like ice skating, a sandwich on the Millennium Wheel or a picnic in a boat on the Serpentine work better than a classic dinner out.' Romance is something that often goes out of a relationship early on; try to keep it alive by making an effort to do things a bit differently. Think about how much it meant at the beginning that your partner had even agreed to go on a date with you. Try to recapture that feeling and hold

on to it; at least for a night once in a while. Increase the sexiness and excitement of being together by doing something you don't normally do. Get on a bargain flight to a city you've never visited, spend all day in bed feeding each other strawberries or do something you've always wanted to do but have never dared try, be it bungee-jumping or dressing up in a nurse's uniform.

Defining idea…

'Variety is the spice of life.'
Late 18th century proverb

If you're not in a regular relationship then try to break out of your own pattern once in a while too. If you normally spend Saturday afternoons watching the football, get off the sofa and go to a museum for once. If you're single, it's an even better idea. 'Museums are a perfect pulling ground,' a 21-year-old male friend tells me. 'They're the one place girls often go alone and you can easily strike up a conversation by asking what they think of a particular painting. And they love the fact that you're there at all, it immediately says you're the sensitive, arty type.'

23. Getting it right

How do you get your lover to love you the way you want to be loved?

Just because you've been together forever, doesn't mean you press each other's buttons absolutely perfectly. Yet the man or woman who can tell their lover that they want to be touched differently from the way they've been touched a million times before is pretty rare.

There are ways to ask without embarrassing yourself and mortifying your lover. Here's how to get your lover to do something differently when they think they've been getting it right for years.

The WRONG way

Using phrases starting with 'Why don't you…', 'You never…' or 'That doesn't…' will cause offence and your partner will get defensive. Moreover, whining is deeply unattractive.

The RIGHT way

Step 1: Praise, praise, praise – your new resolution

From now on, you're going to be an appreciative lover. You're going to praise your lover's performance every chance you get and using every

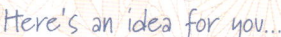

Here's an idea for you...

Always find something positive to say, but don't praise what's bad. Pretending to enjoy what you don't enjoy is what's got you in this mess in the first place!

way you can think of. This will create a 'win–win' situation. Be especially appreciative during sex. Do it with body language. Do it loudly. Spell it out: 'I love everything you do in bed', 'You're just so sexy', 'No one's ever done that to me the way that you do'. They should finish every session assured that you're blissfully happy.

If you're not an appreciative lover, make this your modus operandi from now on. For one thing, this technique will backfire spectacularly on you if it stops as soon as you get what you want – it will look like a cynical ploy. (That's because it will be a cynical ploy.) So wise up, there's nothing to be ashamed of in creating confidence in your lover. Their 'win' is that you're creating an atmosphere where they can't fail. They won't fear trying something different if they don't feel that your happiness is dependent on it. If they get it wrong or if they don't want to go through with it, they've nothing to lose because they know just how much you value them. Your 'win' is that besides being a lovely person you're also gearing them up for moving your sex life on to greater heights.

Step 2: Focus on the positive
Once you've created a climate of confidence, you can modify their technique by focusing on the positive. For instance, 'I love the way you do that, especially when you go slowly/quickly/hang off the bedside

table while you're doing it.' The other great bonus of this approach is that within reason it doesn't matter if it's a complete lie. For example, your lover may go down on you with the speed of a rotodriver, but if you tell him how lovely it is when his mouth goes really slowly he'll probably believe you. He'll almost certainly start doing it slowly too. The payoff for you is that you'll get more of what you want.

Defining idea…

'The secret to telling someone they're the worst lover you've ever had, is…not to. Focus on what you want, not what you don't…Start by focusing on yourself, not your partner's [faults]. Make a list of ten things you want more of in bed, ten things you want less of, and ten new things you'd like to try. You have to know what you want in bed in order to get it.'

TRACEY COX, Supersex

This clearly can be overdone. He's obviously going to get suspicious if he never hangs off the edge of the bedside table while doing it yet you can't stop talking it up. Use discretion and be specific if possible. And you really need to use your hands to gently direct the action the way you want it.

Step 3: Suggest how they could change

Now you can suggest doing it differently. This has to be done with grace and it has to be done lightly, not as if your entire sexual happiness depends on it (remember they can't fail). Say that you've read about something you'd like to try in a book and ask if they would oblige….

24. Lust – it's all in your mind

Not as interested as you used to be? The easiest way out of a rut is to get sex on the brain – literally.

Researching this book has thrown up some surprises for me and one of them has been the effect on my own libido.

Always an 'average' on the sex-o-meter – in other words, I'm not the girl most likely to suggest a love-in with the neighbours – thinking, reading and talking about sex for three months has had an extraordinary effect on my sexual response. I don't mean that I've been tempted to give swinging a try, but having sex on the brain has definitely increased my desire for sex and I'll now advise people that the simplest way to ensure you have (and want) more sex is to think about it more regularly.

As time goes on, we become subsumed in the minutiae of our lives – the fetching, carrying, hunting, gathering. But as sex writer Ann Hooper says, 'You can try every sex position you can think of, including dangling from the ceiling, but if you don't bring your fertile brain into play, you may not manage to become aroused.'

The secret is to fantasise. But first you'll have to rethink your idea of what sexual fantasy means.

Here's an idea for you...

Read sexy romance novels or soft porn. Listen to music that makes you feel sexual – whatever it is, if it rocks your boat, play it loud and play it often.

When did you consistently have the best sex you've ever had? Most of us would say in the first few months of getting it on with a new partner, hopefully the partner we're still with. Why? New love of course, or new lust at the very least. The principal reason that the sex at the beginning of a relationship is so outstanding is that it's fantasy-fuelled. New lovers spend just about every minute they're not in bed with their lover fantasising about their lover. Their minds are constantly running over what they got up to the night before and what they'd like to be doing next time they meet. They walk around in a fug of erotic fantasy. And this fuels their sexual encounters. The second they see their lover they're primed and ready to go.

We tend to think it's the person that fuels our desperation for sex, but physiologically it's got just as much to do with the mind being constantly focused on doing the deed and the signals this sends to our body. So, if you've wistfully looked back on the way you used to feel about each other and if you firmly believe that you can't reconstruct that lust, try thinking about sex more. Any thoughts you have – no matter how fleeting – count. Think about sex during the day, and when the chance to have sex turns up you're far more likely to be enthusiastic. Just a touch will get the juices flowing. On the other hand, if nary a sexual thought has fluttered across your mind during the day, your lover is going to have an uphill and probably futile struggle to get you to even try.

Counsellor Sarah Litvinoff says, 'Sex therapists often find that women who claim never to have been sexually interested or who have gone off sex, never think sexual thoughts. Many people narrowly define sexual fantasies as the mini-pornographic scenes you play out in your head, which might include, say, bondage or lesbian images, that are a mental turn-on, but which you wouldn't necessarily enjoy enacting for real. But, in fact, any sexual thought is sexual fantasy.' And any sort of sexual thought gets the job done.

Let your mind wander, look for the lascivious and feel the throb of sex that is lying beneath the layers of our sophisticated lifestyle. Find stimulation in your daily routine and you'll find yourself overspilling with erotic charge, which will translate into action. You will initiate sex and respond to your partner in a different way sexually. You'll be gagging for it.

Begin to make a habit of daydreaming about sex. First thing when you wake up in the morning or last thing before you go to sleep, think a dirty thought or two. When you're commuting, let the last time you made love run through your mind. As you're queuing or waiting for your train, relive your sexual greatest hits. Remember that every time sex flits across your mind it's a fantasy, and that those who fantasise most have the best sex lives.

NB Like faith healing, you don't have to believe in this for it to work.

Here's an idea for you...

Count the number of people you meet in a day who actively appeal to you. Seek to get aroused by other people, but obviously don't act on it. That old chestnut about taking the energy back to stoke the home fires isn't an old chestnut for nothing.

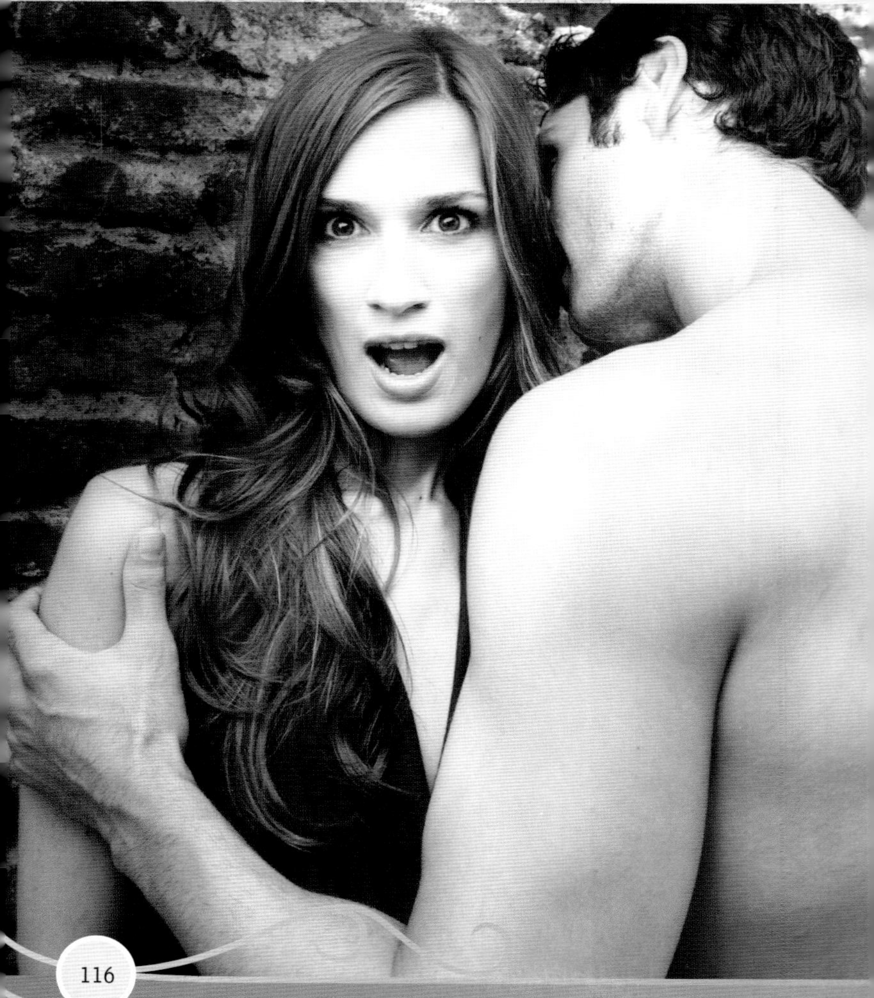

25. Surprise!

Isn't it time you got in touch with your creative side?

Laura Corn, author of '101 Nights of Grrreat Sex', has based her considerable best-selling success on one simple concept: the importance of the surprise factor. Each of her 101 suggestions depends on the fact that your partner doesn't have a clue what sexual delight you're planning.

It's a clever gimmick and it works. Surprise your lover sexually every week for a year and you can bet your bootee you won't be collecting any 'boring in bed' prizes. Encouraging the element of surprise in your sex life will keep you young and playful, keep you feeling cherished and appreciated and keep your lover crazy for you.

A little bit of effort to surprise your lover with a new technique, seduction, outfit or behaviour reaps huge improvements. As long as it's something unexpected, the surprise can be whatever you like. It can be filthy, funny, sweet and romantic or it can be more embarrassing than karaoke night down your local.

Why surprise works

Some of your surprises will be easy to organise. Some will take more planning. You might spend an hour (or more) setting up a gorgeous

Here's an idea for you...

Do something slightly different every time you make love. Throw in an element of surprise. Mixing it up will become second nature after a few weeks and the payoff will make it worthwhile..

seduction for your mate, which is a lot I grant you, but the end result (and this is no exaggeration) will be burned into the hard drive of their memory for the rest of their life. Great sex has that sort of effect on us.

But even more unforgettable for your mate than the great sex you'll enjoy is how loved they'll feel. Men, just as much as women (in fact, if the psychologists are to be believed, even more than women), are delighted by the proof that someone wants them so much that they'll put thought and effort into their seduction. All of us love to feel special.

What does it take for it to work?

It takes both of you to commit to the idea. You will only want to put effort into thrilling your partner if you feel they're going to make the same effort for you.

I recommend Laura Corn's book (mentioned above) because she gives you lots of ideas and she gives you structure. The surprise element can't be spontaneous, at least not at first. If we don't plan, we just get lazy and don't bother. You're aiming to give your lover a 'guaranteed surprise', if you see what I mean. In other words, although they'll be able to look forward to being surprised, they won't know what they're looking forward to.

If you don't want to spring for Corn's book, then in the immortal words of Fleetwood Mac, 'Go your own way.' Or simply customise some of the following suggestions to get the ball rolling:

For her

❀ He's in the shower. Wait until it's good and steamy in there and then slip in beside him wearing your flimsiest, sheerest underwear. If there's one thing more likely to turn him on than you naked, it's wet, clinging wisps of material. (Blokes could try this, too, but it has to be silk boxers – soggy, cotton Y-fronts just don't cut it.)

❀ On your next date, you can keep your coat on. Well, you don't want the whole restaurant to know you're naked underneath. Just him.

For him

❀ Buy her half a case of her favourite wine (a dozen bottles is classier, but might be too much of a demand on your imagination). Around the neck of each, place a sealed envelope containing details of where and when you're going to drink it together. These are IOUs of pleasure. Let your imagination run riot.

✿ One night when you're getting amorous in a lovey-dovey sort of way, suddenly flip personality – change the whole atmosphere. From Dr Jekyll to Mr Hyde. Stop smiling. Get mean. Overcome her. Tie her wrists to the headboard and blindfold her. Now you can do whatever you like, but if you want to give her a night to remember (and especially if she's still really pissed off with you), go down on her until she stops cursing and starts begging.

✿ Spend an hour or so pleasuring her sensually, such as oral sex, washing her hair, painting her toenails, applying body lotion to every inch of her skin or holding her and stroking her hair until she falls asleep. Don't allow her to do a thing for you in return.

121